Frontline Sales Coaching

Paul   Archer

High House Publishing

First published in Great Britain in 2015 by High House Publishing, High House, Priors Norton, Gloucestershire, GL2 9LS, United Kingdom.

Second edition published 2016 by High House Publishing

Printed and bound in Great Britain by Lulu.com.

Copy edited by Shelly Davis

Cover designed by Nirkri

ISBN 978-0-9571738-8-0 (Paperback)

ISBN 978-0-9571738-9-7 (ePub)

For all your sales coaching needs, in-house requirements, contact Paul at

paul@paularcher.com

www.paularcher.com

www.frontlinesalescoaching.com

+44 (0)1452 730276

This book is dedicated to my family and close friends for their inspiration and support. Plus all the salespeople that I've been able to coach over the last 30 years and sales coaches I've had the pleasure of working with.

Table of Contents

Introduction

This book is dedicated to those who want to increase and improve the performance of their sales team and keep them highly motivated and accomplishing beyond expectations.

My focus will be on the frontline, the coal face, being with the salesperson as I believe the sales coach's role is to be with their people at all times--helping them, guiding, supporting, and above all, coaching them.

So if you're the sales coach who likes to drive your desk, handle head office problems, immersing yourself in politics and projects and keeping an eye on your salespeople through a CRM dashboard, then this book is not for you.

But if you're not, then read on and allow me to begin by illustrating what modern sales coaching is and what opportunities we have to practice. I'll relate this to inside sales and face-to-face sales whether you are business-to-consumer (B2C) or business-to-business (B2B).

Because we're focussing on frontline sales coaching, I'm going to examine the four opportunities available for us to coach:

1. Coaching your salesperson's goals and objectives to help them achieve even more
2. Observing sales calls to provide opportunities to give feedback and self-development
3. Performing one-to-one catch-ups to help them improve their performance and develop
4. Demonstrating best practice playbook sales skills

These chapters will discuss process, models, and the "how to" coach, and because I'm lucky enough to work with hundreds of sales-led organisations around the world, everything we talk about does work and will bring results.

I'll then open up the Sales Coach's Toolbox, a metaphorical box of tools that all accomplished coaches can demonstrate in abundance--questioning capability, body language mastery, listening proficiency, the ability to tailor the communication, how to establish rapport, and how to take notes so that the coaching becomes a continued process rather than a one-hit wonder.

I've sprinkled along the journey lots of personal stories and anecdotes to illustrate the concepts and to entertain. By the end of the book, you'll know me and my family quite well.

The Value of Sales Coaching

The 3x3 Role of a Sales Manager

People often ask me to define the role of a sales leader, and we often talk about the usuals, such as recruit, motivate, and so on.

But here's the 3x3 I heard recently which really resonated with me as it's so succinct and obvious:

1. Behaviours – determine them and live them.
2. Value – agree with them and breathe them.
3. Engagement – encourage it amongst the team and do it yourself.

4. Set goals.
5. Communicate the goals.
6. Measure and lead with the goals.

7. Attract good people.
8. Keep the good people.
9. Develop the talent in your people.

And as Forrest Gump once said, "That's all I've got to say about that."

What's the value in coaching?

We've just seen from the 3x3 model that the modern sales leader has nine roles, and from those, three are directly related to coaching.

- Engagement – encourage it amongst the team and do it yourself.

- Keep the good people.

- Develop the talent in your people.

Coaching is not something you turn on when you need to; it's a style of sales managing which we'll discover in more depth in this book, but for now, let's examine the value that coaching creates for you and your sales team.

It's an exercise I often run on my sales coaching workshops. What value does coaching create? However, I run the exercise at the end of the workshop when my budding coaches have discovered how and when they can coach.

Here are some of the responses, in no particular order:

- Improves motivation

- Helps salespeople to "own" development

- Encourages them to be self-sufficient with ideas and steps

- Discourages too much reliance on the sales coach's wisdom

- Shares best practice

- Gives salespeople attention

- Develops their skills on the frontline and prevents "wallowing in theory"

- Is time well-spent

- Allows the coach self-satisfaction of a job well-done.

- Gels a team together

- Ensures compliance with sales process and requirements

- Gets you out of head office

- Improves salesperson's service and engagement

- Is the right way to be

- Keep your people for longer

- Word gets around so you can recruit good people who want to work for you

Unexpected item in bagging area

I started on them two years ago and I have to say they were a nightmare to use. Computer voice telling you off all the time, couldn't find the bar code, authorisation needed, unexpected item in bagging area. Argghh.

But...

Tesco knew this and placed helpful, smiley people around them to answer any query, and these people were specially trained to be unflappable against the frustrations of shoppers. They were happy to show you how to use the machines and would encourage you and answer your questions. Always available and on hand.

Two years later, completely different story. People flow through the self-service area like water through a pipe. We all know instinctively what to do and might even enjoy the speed advantage it gives you. And there's always someone keeping a beady eye in case they're needed.

Bit like on-the-job coaching really. Whenever a new system comes in or a new product, do you flood your sales force with coaches trained to answer questions, guide, and be unflappable when the salesperson gets frustrated with the new system? Tesco did, and although their profits are down this year, their salesperson care is up. Clever Tesco, that's what I say, differentiating themselves from a crowded commodity-based marketplace.

Fix your injured player for a competitive advantage

I was reading in the paper about how two football teams, neck-and-neck at the top of the Premiership on points, who had completely different medical facilities for fixing injured players. As a result, the team who just seems to keep winning the Premiership is able to help players recover far quicker and with more sustainability than the other team. And this has given them a competitive advantage, and that are pretty rare these days.

The parallels for a sales team are enormous.

Manchester United has used an underwater treadmill initially designed for NASA called the HydroWorx Underwater Treadmill to bring Antonio Valencia back from a broken ankle incurred in September 2010, and he is looking a better, fitter player as a result.

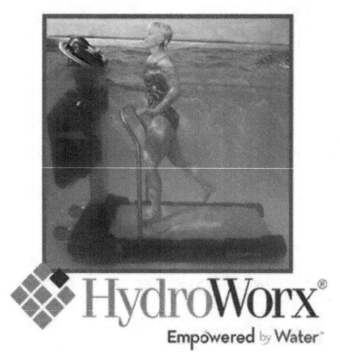

The parallels. Your salespeople get injured and need fixing. I'm not referring to injuries and bone breakages like Valencia; I'm talking about drops in confidence, suddenly lacking key skills, a need for new knowledge, more attention. Do you have state-of-the-art facilities to recuperate the lost confidence and rebuild the skills and knowledge so the salesperson gets back on the road better and fitter than before?

If you do, then you'll have a competitive advantage.

Can you see why a player's performance has dipped? And can you help them improve through coaching or counselling or good old-fashioned training? The danger is to try and fix them too quickly and put them back on the road as soon as possible. This is a mistake, as Arsenal is finding out.

The more expensive your players, the more talented and skilled they are, the more sophisticated needs to be your recovery methods, and a football parallel with players earning millions just might help us find the investment for our salespeople.

But the Premiership isn't won yet. There are still a few games to go, but perhaps having Valencia backfiring on all cylinders might give United the edge needed to win.

Minor gains are the coach's aim

My eldest son is taking his driving test soon after nine months of arduous and stressful driving lessons.

We forget how difficult learning to drive was; we take it for granted now that we've been road warriors for many years. But when you learn to drive, you improve by inches.

Each week, you improve on one small aspect. It might be reversing, changing gear from two to three, turning left at a junction, the hill start. Each improvement gradually builds your capability to drive, and a good driving instructor knows implicitly which competency to develop at any given time.

In the same way, as sales coaches, we need to be skilled at recognising which area needs cultivating in order to build long-term capability. It's all about small improvements. Sir Dave Brailsford from the Sky British Cycling Team calls it incremental gains, and his boys keep winning the Tour de France.

So carry out regular coaching and work on small things, one at a time. Look for priorities, not spectacular gains, and let your salespeople develop at the same pace as a learner driver.

And treat experienced salespeople the same. They get into bad habits as do experienced drivers. I know I do.

What is Sales Coaching?

The Definitive Definition of Coaching

How can a car breakdown illustrate perfectly modern coaching in the workplace?

Let me explain my son's little debacle last night.

On his way back from work at around eleven p.m., Lewis turned into our lane and the clutch blew. He stopped the car, put on the hazard lights, and called home.

He was in a state, as you can imagine. He's nineteen and has never broken down before. He had no idea what to do, no frame of reference to cope with the situation, although he did fine by parking it in the lay-by and putting on the hazard lights.

So I took control. No coaching, just control and direction.

Two hours later we were all walking back to the house, the car was in a better place, and I called the breakdown people to tow it to the garage. Apart from a rather large and juicy garage bill coming my way, everything was organised and all were safe.

As we walked up the lane, I went into coaching mode because I wanted Lewis to start taking ownership.

"How are you getting to work tomorrow, Lewis?"

"I dunno, Dad."

"Have a think about it, Lewis…"

"Can you give me a lift, Dad?"

"Sorry, Lewis, I'm working myself – any ideas?"

I went quiet; he thought about it.

"I guess I'll have to get the bus. I'll look up the timetable tonight on my phone."

"Sounds like a good plan, Lew. What about late at night, when the bus isn't running?"

"Can you pick me up?"

"Yep, I can do that."

"Fine," said Lewis.

Coaching, pure and simple. My intentions were for Lewis to own his journey, have responsibility for his decisions, and know the consequences of his actions. Coaching does that, and I used the GROW model as structure. We'll talk about the GROW process later.

As for the car, I'm waiting to hear from the garage how much it'll cost. I'm dreading it!

Are you a coach, a mentor, or a tormentor?

I heard a phrase the other day that stuck with me.

Is your sales manager a coach, a mentor, or a tormentor?

More importantly, as a sales manager yourself, do you regard yourself as a coach, mentor, or tormentor? I'm sure you don't regard yourself as the latter, but do check with your people just in case.

Here's a little checklist to test to see that you're not tormenting your team.

1. Do you promise to coach but frequently run out of time, or other priorities take precedence and you're always apologetic?
2. Do you find yourself managing your team purely through KPIs and other stats, and much of the time you just email them to your salesperson and ask for their comments?
3. If a salesperson's results are down, do you email them at the end of the week for a telephone conversation to talk about the numbers?
4. Do you constantly promote competition amongst your sales team?
5. In sales meetings do you find much of the time is spent with each salesperson talking about their week/month in sales?

Only a short questionnaire, but if you found yourself answering more of these with yes rather than no, then you may be deemed as a tormentor even though you had no intention of this whatsoever but just lack time.

Don't double the self-talk when coaching

Sometimes I think wives are also replacement mothers for their husbands. I know because my wife is. She cares so much, that when I'm away on a business trip, she'll always keep reminding me:

"Don't forget two shirts, underwear for three days. Remember to take your washbag. You forgot once, didn't you? Alarm clocks, remember those, some nuts in the car in case you get hungry."

The only problem with this is that I've been travelling on business since 1989 and consider myself a road warrior, so I have my own routines and schedules to ensure I remember things. I say to myself things like:

"Okay, Paul, you're away three nights, so that's three shirts plus ties, belt, two suits, washbag. Put something to eat in the car in case…"

And hey, presto, I've got two voices in my head. One from me and one from my "coach", and I get all confused and mixed up with two voices talking to me from inside my head.

And as a coach, this is a dangerous place to be for your coachees and a prime reason why, as coaches, we mustn't ever tell our coachees what to do. If we do, we'll double their talk.

The best self-talk has to come from the coachee's head in their own voice. So, when coaching, just make sure you ask questions that encourage them to figure things out, to work out the answers. Don't put "tells" into their head; just ask questions to help them create the inner dialogue. That way they'll only have one voice, not yours, ringing in their heads.

And that's what I have, my wife's voice ringing in my head as I leave, which is wonderful really because I know she cares. Well, I think she cares. She does rather like it when I'm away. The house seems to run much smoother when I'm not there. Maybe she just likes giving me advice when I go away to encourage me to be away a whole lot more. Hmmm, I wonder…

Coaching and Your Satnav (GPS)

With a family funeral in the New Forest, we had a need to travel the two-hour journey from Gloucestershire to Hampshire on many occasions. On one return journey, I asked my nineteen-year-old son if he felt comfortable to make the journey himself.

"I could, Dad, but I'd have to have a satnav (GPS)."

"Yes, Lewis, they do help enormously, but once upon a time we used to make journeys like this without them."

"Like last century, Dad."

We drifted back into silence, and I started to think about what would happen if we didn't have satellite navigation in our cars.

And that made me think because not so long ago, I would use Google Maps to plot my route and imagine it through in my head, making a mental note of junctions and directions. When I was on the road, I would relate my previous thinking to the current route, checking road signs and keeping an eye on my milometer and the time.

We were much more focussed on the actual route and concentrated more.

And we'd arrive safely enough with a copy of the map on the passenger seat just in case.

I thought to myself that satnavs replace all of this. They make us lazy, reliant on others, i.e. the software, and we have no ownership of the route.

In the same way, this is exactly what sales coaching does. As coaches, we ask questions and help our coachees to think things through in the same way we'd think through the route the night before. We don't tell the coachees what to do and how to do it. We help them figure it out and own the final solution. Satnavs tell us what to do, and we become so reliant on them.

How awful would it be if the satnav stopped working in mid-flight? How would we cope?

Lewis asked me that same question, and my horrific response motivated me to buy a £2.99 map-book at my next petrol stop.

The Coaching Swingometer

My first role as a trainee manager for a bank in the 1980s exposed me to the traditional hierarchical management style that predominated. My manager's office stood high above us and overlooked our working area. He had huge internal windows which enabled him to glare at us all day without leaving the sanctuary of his room.

How things have changed, and rightfully so.

Today, successful managers operate a coaching style, continually developing their teams and unleashing their people's ability and skills. Coaching is particularly effective at developing people, discarding the reliance on classroom training and putting development on the job, where it belongs.

One barrier I have witnessed in many companies I've worked with is the manager's confusion as to what coaching is and how it can be used as the ultimate tool for developing people. Everyone has their opinion, but most agree that pure coaching is where the team member has all the answers, has the ability, and once made aware, determines their own solutions. This fits very well in a textbook but not so well in a bustling, stressful, deadline-oriented retail salesperson facing environment. Here, we want more flexibility, indirect and direct coaching. Let me show you the Coaching Swingometer.

Made famous by the BBC, their election Swingometer found out how vote swings between political parties could affect the outcome of the general election.

Presenter Robert McKenzie with the swingometer on election night, 1964 © BBC

In the same way, our coaching Swingometer can plot the person you're coaching and can help you decide the variety of coaching that should be used given the situation you're facing. Let me explain.

Here is the Coaching Swingometer.

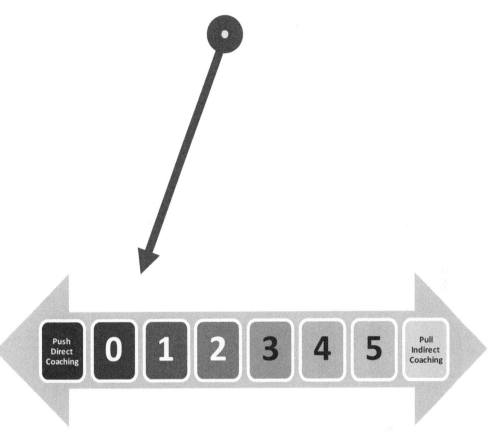

On the left side of the Swingometer is direct coaching or push coaching, which is tell mode coaching, more one-to-one training than coaching, suitable when the team member wants some help or guidance or needs to be shown how something works or how to speak with a salesperson or handle an irate salesperson.

As we move to the right, we let go as coaches, encouraging more responsibility and awareness with our team member, helping them to decide their next steps. We use feedback tools to help the team member develop. We support their decisions, use tools such as GROW, and head towards indirect coaching or pull coaching.

The Swingometer can swing during one coaching session. For example a team member comes to you asking for some help on handling a particularly irate salesperson in the foyer. It's so easy to brush them aside and go and pacify the salesperson yourself. But good coaching empowers the team member by unlocking their ability to handle the situation. You might start your instant coaching session by giving them some pointers and ideas, and follow up with a question as to how they're going to handle the salesperson, what they are going to say, and empower them that way.

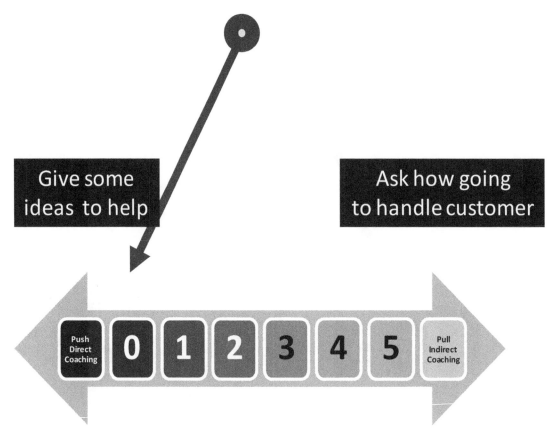

Another example is a new programme on the system. You start by doing some one-to-one training in the branch with your team member, showing them how it works, demonstrating. Then you might follow up with some mock exercises and ask how they're going to use the system to help them give better service to our salesperson.

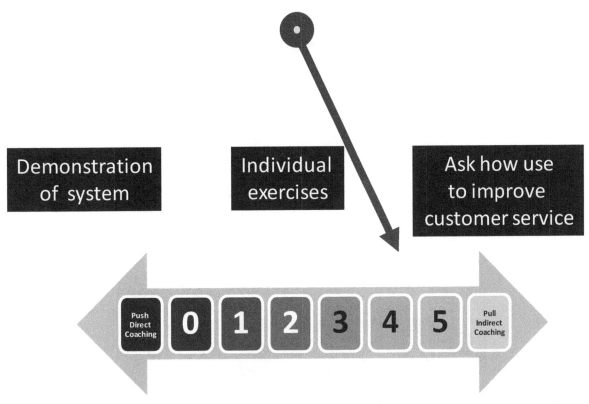

You might be conducting one-on-one with a team member to determine their learning goals for the following quarter. Here you would go straight to the right-hand side of the Coaching Swingometer and operate the GROW model in a purely indirect fashion, so they completely own the decisions they make.

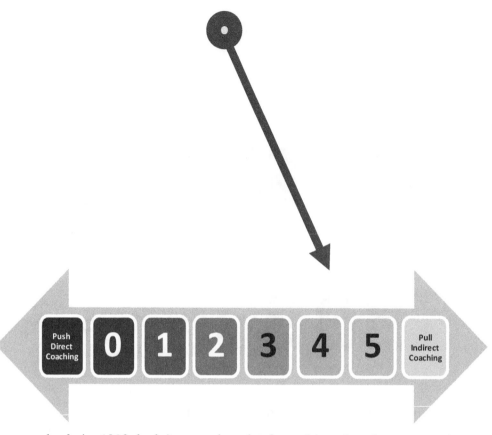

My manager back in 1983 hadn't even heard of coaching, let alone any other style of management. To a degree, neither had we, the team members. But teams have changed in the 2010s. The majority of people working in sales, facing retail environments, are Generation Y's and late Generation X's. These generations know about coaching or its components and seek out an inclusive, empowering management style. They were brought up by parents who involved them in all family decisions, and they need this culture to continue in the workplace. These generations have all the information at their fingertips they could dream of, so probably know more than their manager. They want to be able to use it practically and continually learn and develop on the job.

Our teams have changed; so must we, and the Coaching Swingometer can help you determine the style of coaching you operate for any eventuality in a salesperson-facing environment.

The power of self-awareness questions

Self-awareness questions were the first coaching technique I learnt when being trained to coach in 1993. I had no idea what Frank was going on about. Frank was our trainer, by the way.

How on earth could you teach or coach people through self-awareness questions? Nonsense, I thought. I guess I struggled at the time to distinguish between the two – coach and train.

But last Sunday I had to make self-awareness coaching work, otherwise I was doomed, destined to the ranks of a third-rate rugby coach with my Under 14's team.

Head Coach Mark asked me to take away our two scrum-halfs and do some personal coaching with them. Crikey, I thought. In my rugby-playing days I never went near the scrum-halfs, preferring the sanctuary of the rucks and mauls. And I still haven't the faintest idea how they do their job.

So I had to think quickly on my feet.

One of our scrum-halfs, Jakey, is particularly good, and another one was learning the ropes, so I immediately got Jakey to show Dan some of his best moves.

Brilliant. But then it was my turn to coach them both…so I started asking self-awareness questions, questions simply designed to get them to express what they are doing, what they're observing, feeling, touching…so they become more aware and conscious of how to do it better—tweaking the finer points.

"So, Jakey, what technique are you using there?"

"Who are you watching when you pass the ball?"

"What position are your feet in as you reach down?"

And so on. Soon Dan took over, and I continued to ask the same questions.

"Dan, where are you looking now?"

"Dan, what angle are you holding the ball?"

Phew, I thought to myself as the two boys improved their game. *"Thanks, Coach,"* they said at the end. *"That was cool."*

The power of self-awareness questions. But has it taken me eighteen years to figure them out? I don't know, but without them last Sunday, I would have become a third-rate junior rugby coach. At least I remain second-rate, one day maybe first-rate!

9 Reminders of What Great Coaching is

Match vigorously

Becoming like them will lubricate communication. Listen and use their language and key words. Note how much emphasis is put on their words and use these yourself. Some coaches note down just the key words on paper to use later.

Naturally you mirror their physiology, their energy, eye contact. What about pace and tone of voice, hand gestures, but only when you talk.

Create Presence

Start with a relaxed and open state, no barriers. When this state has been created, bottle the energy bubble and cloak it. Place the cloak over the two of you and this will allow you to block out any distractions even in a busy hotel bar.

Sharing your ideas

Many new coaches or very busy coaches find it painful to wait patiently and let their ideas percolate. Instead they like to give their ideas or opinions. Strictly speaking this is dangerous as the ideas become yours, not theirs and they become reliant on you. Leading questions are even more painful; just don't go there. Here's a few ideas:

Challenge a different person to come out with some ideas – how would your playful self answer or how would your mentor respond?

Mentally step out of the coaching bubble and offer your idea but give them an opt out clause. Let's step out of our coaching session for a moment as I've a couple of ideas to float past you. If they're not fruitful we'll go somewhere else.

"Can I offer you my line of thinking?"

"What would a courageous you say?"

"Let's step out for a moment, I do have an idea."

Then give them the opt out.

Would that work for you? If that's not a rich seam for you, where else would you want to go?

Read physiology, sense and challenge

Calibrate them immediately and observe leakage, when you see it, challenge it. For example, with a sudden sweep of the arms, ask if they want to move on or sweep away the idea. Watch their face closely and look for expression leaks and challenge them.

Endless curiosity

Which translates into brilliant listening, which all coaches do. It's not about active listening, it's about being in the present, not judging or solving the problem prematurely in your head. It's about being curious to find out more. Clear the mind, trust in your ability to listen and stop thinking. That's their job, not yours.

Truly wonderful coaches then summarise regularly. 25% of coaches summarise a little and paraphrase a lot. 25% of coaches just test their understanding but 50% of coaching effectiveness comes from doing both – summarising regularly and testing your understanding: *"Have I got that right?" "Is that where we are?"*

Mature questioning flexibility

Good coaches do ask short open questions with lots of sugar coating – using tone of voice and softeners such as – *"Tell me"*, or *"I'd be curious to know"*. Excellent coaches use a variety of question types in a funnel approach. Broad questions at the top of the funnel to light the fire, probes to keep them on the subject, closed questions to channel thinking and confirm.

Well paid coaches then stoke the fire. Tease conversation from them, never ever interrogate. Coaching is about asking questions but not continuously. Use your senses to channel, play devil's advocate, enjoy silence, let them think things through, watch their eye movement as this will show thinking. Give them space. Use nods both verbal and non-verbal to encourage their talk. Empathy statements work in showing an understanding of their conversation.

Actions that'll be actioned

We've all seen coaches using the words – *"I'll better do this"* or *"I ought to do it this way by next week or I'll be in trouble"*. When action planning at the end of the session – when, what, whom – test their dependability. On a scale of one to ten, how likely are you to do this? What do we need to do to get this nearer a ten?

Listen out for their motivational state – is it duty, drive or flow? Do they have to do it, do they need to do it or do they want to do it? – Flow.

Elicit strategies

Everyone with a few miles on their clock will have strategies to do things: methods or structures to handle most aspects of their lives. I call these strategies. So in the reality stage of the GROW model, explore how they would normally handle this kind of goal. How do they normally make decisions, what strategies do they normally use to brainstorm?

Belief systems around goals

During the reality stage, most coaches will explore what the person has done before, the current situation. Great coaches explore the belief system surrounding the topic since beliefs determine the action they'll take. Probe around their supporting and restraining beliefs. What's important to you around this topic? How do you feel about it? What do you believe around this area?

When Should We Coach?

The true role of a sales manager

I'd like you to think back to your last holiday. Now that's a gorgeous memory, isn't it? Can you recall the holiday rep who was there to take care of things for you? I can, from our holiday in France last year. Let me share with you how David's performance was so close to how sales managers should be operating.

Now David, our holiday rep on our French campsite holiday, was a breath of fresh air. The typical rep is out to sell you excursions, clean your accommodations, and make sure you leave on time. A little harsh, but you get my point. But this year we had someone who knew exactly what his role was, and was keen to tell me:

"My role, Paul, is to make sure every guest of our holiday firm has a great time. I want them all to enjoy their stay, have some fond memories, and want to come back. If they have a great time, they'll say good things about me to the head office, and that helps me. I'm targeted on our clients having a great time."

That simply was what he did – everything he did was towards helping us have a great time. He didn't have to crunch numbers and achieve targets; he wasn't relaying orders and direction from head office, counting the number of caravans occupied and reporting back those that weren't. He didn't have to requisition new equipment for the accommodations, or report breakages or damage. He didn't have to remain in his office on the telephone to HQ firefighting and solving problems. No, his job was to make sure we all had a great time.

And this got me thinking about the role of a sales manager. I think their role is to help their salespeople sell more. Not to be in the office, firefighting, watching metrics and sales results, and reporting new targets and objectives.

No, the role of the sales manager is to help the salesperson sell more by coaching, sharing best practices, training salespeople, dual calling, helping with big accounts, and giving sales ideas freely.

Just like David in France.

Developing your people model

The "Developing Your People" model is concerned with helping you to do the right thing at the right time as a sales coach.

Adopting the right methods and behaviours according to a person's competence and self-reliance seems fairly straightforward, but too often sales coaches fail to get the best out of people because they unthinkingly adopt the wrong approach.

The usual problems that sales coaches face can be summed up as either "letting go too soon" or "not letting go at all". In other words, the sales coach credits the staff member with far more competence and self-reliance than he had actually got. Or, he fails to recognise that the staff member has developed beyond a "hands-on" approach.

The model will help you address where each of your team stands in terms of his/her development needs, and what strategy you might employ in response.

The model

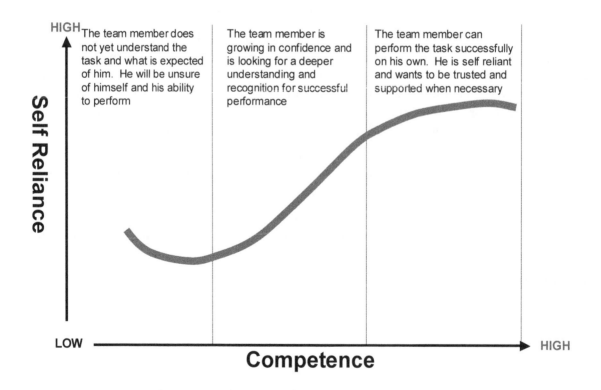

HIGH
The team member does not yet understand the task and what is expected of him. He will be unsure of himself and his ability to perform

The team member is growing in confidence and is looking for a deeper understanding and recognition for successful performance

The team member can perform the task successfully on his own. He is self reliant and wants to be trusted and supported when necessary

Self Reliance

LOW

Competence

HIGH

How to deal

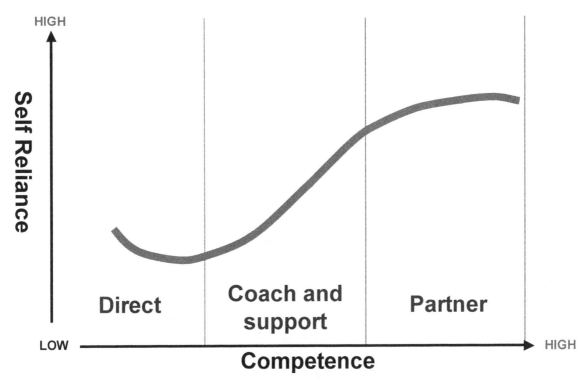

Coaching and mentoring

Coaching is often confused with mentoring. In fact, sometimes the terms are used interchangeably. There are areas of overlap, but there is an important distinction. A mentor is usually an expert in a particular field and works with more junior practitioners in that field, helping them to gain knowledge, skills, and experience.

Coaching is about facilitating self-directed learning and development. The coach does not necessarily have specific expertise in the area of influence of the person he or she is coaching. Sometimes not having expertise in the working area of an individual allows a valuable insight. As one executive coach puts it:

"When I come from the position of being an expert, it's almost as if I have to defend my position. But when you say to yourself, 'I'm not the expert,' even though you may have all this knowledge, it feels more open and you can play around with those ideas. It means I pay more attention. It becomes more active than defensive. It's very powerful."

Coaching and training

Training is about teaching particular skills. It is often a fixed process – a certain number of employees are required to learn a specific set of skills. Unfortunately, the transfer of skills learned on the training course to the workplace tends to be rather low. Studies have also shown that coaching used in conjunction with training can make the training much more effective.

Coaching and consulting

Consultants tend to be experts in their area. Coaches are experts in facilitating learning and goal attainment. Consultants are expected to come up with a model for change, based on information gleaned from the current state of the organisation. They will tend to go into an organisation, suggest a solution, and then leave. Coaches help the individual to find their own solutions. Consultants tend to work with information, processes, and procedures. Coaches work with individuals, relationships, and interpersonal skills. Consultants tell – coaches ask the right questions.

Coaching, counselling, and therapy

Coaching is not therapy, but it does use some techniques derived from clinical psychology. Coaching deals with individuals who are functional, often people who are performing very well indeed. Coaching is less about unravelling problems and difficulties and more about building solutions and improving performance.

The four frontline coaching opportunities

I said earlier that sales coaching is a style of managing, not necessarily something you can turn on and off. However, I want to relate coaching to frontline activities in this book, those activities that are pivotal to the development and success of the salesperson. And it's these that I want to discuss in the next four chapters. These are:

Coaching your salesperson's goals and objectives

This coaching situation can occur anytime. Your salesperson might phone you with a question or problem for you to solve. Coaching can be used here to help them figure it out. You might be in a formal meeting and you want to help them with their current goals. You may be in the middle of an observed sales call day and they have a question, or they need to work out a different way of doing something that you fed back on earlier. The tool here is GROW.

Observed sales calls

Highly effective sales coaches continuously "rise shotgun" with their salespeople, either face-to-face or side-by-side if they're using video technology or the phone to speak with their salesperson. This coaching situation allows you to hear them, observe them, and compare their performance with your best practice or your sales playbook. It allows you to provide motivational feedback and to coach them to think of ways of selling differently. The tools here are SPAM and GROW.

The Sales One-to-One

Sitting down eye-to-eye, belly button-to-belly button with your salesperson in private to discuss their performance and progress. Weekly, monthly, half yearly – every company I work with has different frequencies. The tools here are varied – AID, FISH, GROW, SPELL. All can be used.

Demonstrating Sales Skills

This is more training than coaching, but it's on the job and very tactical, which is why good coaches do it with their salespeople. Coaching can drift over to "push" as long as it doesn't stay there. Role-play, real-life demonstrating, in a classroom, in the car – lots of variety. The tools here are MEDIC and SPAM.

Coaching Your Salesperson's Objectives and Goals

The GROW model

You've probably heard of the GROW coaching model, which is ubiquitous in business. According to the authors of *The Reflecting Glass*, Graham Alexander originated the GROW model in the mid-'80s, but it didn't attract a lot of public attention until it appeared in the first (1992) edition of *Coaching for Performance* by John Whitmore. Max Landsberg also describes GROW in his excellent book, *The Tao of Coaching*.

Enough of the references, I use it a lot; it's practical and more importantly, tactical too. It works. It produces awareness of the issue and responsibility for the action plan, which John Whitmore emphasised in his book more than the actual GROW model. It gives you structure although it's certainly not linear; you can go backwards and forwards as much as you like. And it's simple too.

How do we actually structure a coaching session? The GROW (Goal, Reality, Options)

It's all about asking the right questions so that people:

* Find their own answers

* Take responsibility for the way forward

* Increase their awareness of the reality of the current situation and the possibilities for solutions

The framework provides a simple four-step structure for a coaching session.

* Goal

* Reality

* Options

* Will (or way forward)

Let's take a look at the GROW framework in detail.

Goal

The coach starts to find out about the goal or the objective that the salesperson has. This could be a problem that needs solving. It can be large, possibly more of a topic – some people teach TGROW, where T stands for topic, which is then broken down into smaller goals.

All salespeople have goals, numbers to achieve, metrics to stretch, KPIs to be reached. They also have other goals – to improve closing skills, to be more effective at prospecting, to master social media selling. They might want to improve their time management or be promoted to your job.

The situation determines the goals. You could be running a performance meeting; you could be observing a live sales meeting where you want to see what skill area they're developing; it might be an annual appraisal and you're talking about their career aspirations.

Good coaches will question the goal, not its viability. I don't think we can play God here, but look at how well-formed it is. I talk about SMART and Well-Forming a little later.

Once you have a bite-sized goal to chew on, continue with the remainder of GROW.

Reality

The current reality is where the client is now. What are the issues, the challenges? How far are they away from their goal? What have they done so far in achieving the goal? What has worked and what hasn't? It's pretty much a snapshot of where they currently are.

In a sales situation you could be observing their selling in action, either live or role-play, and you can see where they are now, what their current performance is. For example, they might be working on their pre-closing and you notice a distinct lack of closing throughout the client meeting. Your questions that you ask will allow the salesperson to revisit this in their head. You may need to play back what you saw and heard in your observation so they become crystal clear on their current reality surrounding the goal.

Options

This is normally the longest part of the coaching session, a chance for the salesperson to think through how they can accomplish the goal. What alternative course of action can they take? What are the consequences, the advantages and disadvantages of this route? Who can they speak with? What blogs can they read? What YouTube videos might help? What can you do to help maybe, but I would be wary of offering any ideas or advice.

Novice coaches do this and people I've just trained – they seem desperate to want to offer a solution or two. Premature Solutioneering I call it.

Will (or way forward)

Time now to sift through all the ideas and avenues and pin them down to an action plan that you can help them achieve or they can do themselves. Coaching isn't coaching without actions. Coaching is generative. They need to own the action plan, otherwise it's pretty worthless. This is the crux of coaching – awareness and responsibility for the actions on the salesperson's behalf.

GROW example questions

Goal

- What does the person you are coaching want to achieve?
- What is the aim of this discussion?
- What do you want to achieve in the long-term?
- How much personal control or influence do you have over your goal?
- What is the short-term goal?
- When do you want to achieve it by?

Reality

- What's happening now in relation to the goal, and what's happened that's relevant in the past?
- What's happening now?
- What/when/where/how much/how often?
- Who's involved?
- When things are going badly on this issue, what happens to you?
- What happens to those who are directly involved?
- What have you done about it so far?
- What results did that produce?
- What are the major constraints to find a way forward?

Options

- What can the person you are coaching do?

- What options do you have?

- What else could you do?

- What if……..(there was more/less time/budget, etc.)?

- What are the benefits and costs of each?

Will

- What will the person do?

- What are they prepared to commit to?

- What are you going to do?

- Will this address your goal?

- What could arise to inhibit this action?

- How will you overcome this?

- What support do you need?

- How will you get that support?

Humility in goal-setting

Waiting in the Emirates lounge on my way home from Dhaka, I made a new friend. His name was Ali, and he was serving refreshments to guests and he made me feel humble.

He was an expert in rapport building—engaging in conversation, finding things that we had in common, both brought up as Catholics, for example.

But what made me think was, when he asked where I was heading and I replied, "London."

"Ah, London, a fine city I think," always complimentary, which is the Bangladeshis' way.

"Have you been?" was my little thought-through reply. I had only recently risen from my bed and it was early.

"No, sir, but I would love to go, but I am from a poor family."

"Make it your goal," I said with my speaker's hat on.

"Pray for me then, sir, and I will achieve my goal."

And that made me think. We all know about goal-setting and how we should choose a great big, hairy, and audacious goal. However, I believe we ought to take stock and see what we have achieved and put it all into perspective.

Humility came to me that moment, from my new friend Ali in Dhaka airport.

Making goals the right size

For most people, the fear of failure is the overriding concern preventing them from making well-formed goals. One issue is that the goal may seem out of reach. A good example is that of a sales adviser who enters the financial services industry and wants to be the very best performer within six months.

The opposite is also true. A goal might seem trivial and so not worth doing or may be relegated to the bottom of the list. Can you think of any examples? An adviser needing to sort through her paperwork, tidy the desk, write a report, or make a phone call. We call this procrastination.

An answer that Neuro Linguistic Programming (NLP) gives is the idea of chunking up and chunking down.

Chunking up

When a goal is too small, simply ask yourself the question:

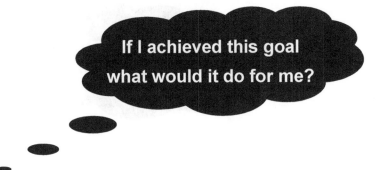

If I achieved this goal what would it do for me?

This steps the goal up to a higher level to reveal more compelling reasons for undertaking the tasks necessary to achieve the goal.

Chunking down

This is particularly useful when a goal seems frustratingly out of reach. Chunking down doesn't eliminate the original goal; it breaks it down into manageable chunks.

Ask yourself:

This question will throw us a number of problems. Take each problem in turn, and ask yourself:

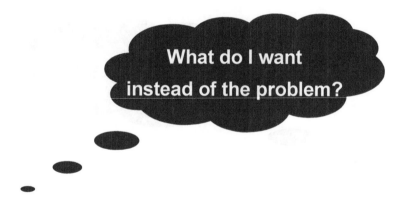

This question will turn problems into smaller goals.

Compelling Outcomes

I'm sure you've heard the phrase "compelling outcomes". It stems from the study of Neuro Linguistic Programming (NLP) and turns the old topic of goal-setting on its head.

The main premise is that traditional goal-setting begins at the start line and talks about setting the future direction. Let's keep goal-setting in this way as it has to start somewhere, but where I'm coming from today is to see your goal from the position of actually achieving it.

Imagine that you have achieved your goal and are able to look back at it being achieved.

In this way, we're able to fully visualise achieving the goal, feel what it feels like, hear what success sounds like, and make the whole goal far more compelling than it appears on paper at the start.

Future pacing

The phrase future pacing rears its head here. It means taking your thoughts to a future event. I used to love doing this during my NLP training – closing my eyes and drifting along my timeline until I reached the event, dropping out of my timeline and slipping into a future event, really feeling that I was actually there.

It took some practice to do, but once you get over the "nerdy" element of hypnosis and imagining the future…then you're on a roll.

I enjoyed the time travel element and being able to let loose with my imagination. After all, it's my mind, and no one else knows what I'm doing.

Pacing your goals

One goal that I set in 1997 and vividly future paced came in for real in late 2000. I can still vividly see the goal being achieved in my tiny office in my old house—a great feeling and proof that it really worked. So let me show you how it works and how it might just take your goal-setting or compelling outcomes to a new level.

A great little acronym to help you in making your goals more compelling is PACES. It stands for:

- Positive
- Achievement
- Control
- Effect
- Step into the future

The idea is to take one of your goals. Any one will do. Maybe one you're struggling to achieve, which is a fairly meaty one too. I'm going to take a goal I set myself at the beginning of the year to help show you how it works. It's a goal that many of you might share, particularly around the beginning of the year.

My goal is to get into shape!

Positive

Phrasing your goal in a negative sense can be self-defeating. Telling your brain not to do something is neither inspiring or practical.

If I said to myself, "Don't put any more weight on Paul," it would send my brain into spasms and I'd not get anywhere. In fact, I would probably start thinking about putting on weight first because to think about not putting any more weight on, I have to think about gaining it first, and this might be what I might do first.

Not good.

No, instead I phrase it as a positive forward sentence, such as, "I need to get into shape." It gives me something to aim for and something to strive towards.

Achievement

Many people talk about making your goals SMART. I'm sure you've heard of this before as it's been doing the rounds for decades now and is pretty clever or smart in its own right.

Specific, measurable, achievable, realistic, and time-bound. SMART works really well with business-type objectives, and I would definitely suggest you use it when you've broken your goal down in to bite-sized chunks.

But for meaningful, compelling outcomes, it doesn't work.

Instead take yourself up into your timeline and whizz off into the future to a time when you had achieved it. Try to imagine the moment as vividly as you can. Now, hold on, have you really got this timeline thing cracked?

First of all, ask yourself, where does my future point? For many people it's straight ahead slightly curved upwards to their right. This is the direction that most people look for their future thoughts, their imagination, and their creativity. But you might be different – it doesn't really matter. What you do need to do is to know where your future timeline goes.

Now imagine yourself whizzing along the timeline. Personally I head up to the skies first and then zoom along the timeline. When I reach the moment, I stop, look down, and there I am in the picture. I flow downwards and settle on the ground and can see myself quite clearly.

It's here that you need to see what it looks like to achieve the goal. What do you see around you? What do you hear? Who else is there? What are you looking like? What expression do you have? Where are you? Now step into your body like one of those 1950s alien movies where the baddies arrive on the Planet Earth and take over human bodies. Now you are yourself. How are you feeling? What's in your mind? What can you see?

A little bit quirky, I can imagine you might be feeling, but if you do this well and practice it, you'll soon be able to know exactly what it's like to achieve the goal.

For the record, my future timeline in is August this year on the French Vendee beach of Brétignolles sur Mer, which has an enormous stretch of white sand.

It's early in the morning. We're on holiday. The family is still snoozing, and I'm running along the sand without a care in my mind. I'm feeling quite fit for a forty-six-year-old, looking reasonable, drifting along the white sands, and looking forward to croissants and marmalade for breakfast.

Before you go any further, try to imagine your goal being achieved at the end of your timeline.

Control

Put simply, can you make the goal happen yourself? Are you in control or are you relying on someone else or something else achieving it for you?

My goal is easy, not to achieve might I add, but easy under this category because I'm in control here. It's my self-motivation that's involved, not a lot else.

But your goal might not be down to you. For example, you might want to be able to motivate your sales team better. Fine, your own skills can be improved in this area, but you also need the right team for them to be motivated. Some people are impossible to motivate.

Effect

What's the effect of you achieving your goal on everyone else around you? Does it fit your life and the people around you? For example, a goal to make £250,000 this year is fine, but if you're working all the hours and never get to see your family until Christmas night, that might not be in keeping with who you are.

My goal of getting into shape can be achieved because it fits who I am and what I'm about, but I need to be careful that I'm not out all the time in the gym, ignoring my family and having special diet menus at a separate time so I don't enjoy family meals. That wouldn't be fair to my family or me.

Make sure the goal is in keeping.

Finally…

Step into the Future

This is my favourite, and I've already mentioned it a few times already. Jump onto your timeline, whiz along it, and find the moment when you've achieved it. Remember, you've already been there so going there again will be easy.

But this time you need to slow down on your way back because I'm going to ask you to see what milestones you crossed as you achieved your goal. Have a look down to see what you're doing along the timeline and make a note of these because they'll become your action steps needed to achieve your goal.

For me, I can see speed walking with my dog Brody along the meadows during January and February at dusk. March, April, and May sees me running along the meadows as it gets drier and lighter in the evening. June and July I start running in the wheat fields near our house in the paths made by the tractors as these become like running tracks, and finally, in August as we head out to France, I can see myself running along those gorgeous strips of sand in France.

Stretching your Goals

Stretch yourself when writing your goals. Just enough to make it a challenge, but don't stretch too far – that's when we pull our backs. Seriously, though, you'd be amazed what humans are capable of when we set our minds to it.

For my fortieth birthday, my wife bought for me a three-hour excursion with a police traffic officer in his excessively fast Volvo. Was I excited? The first lesson was how to control a car whilst skidding, then he taught us how to drive really fast. The finale of the lesson was to take the wheel of his hideously fast Volvo and drive as fast as I could along a public motorway. I tell you, I was scared.

A friend of mine came along to keep me company, and this was great as we could make mistakes together and not feel so bad. But to make a mistake when driving at more than a hundred miles per hour on a public highway could be dangerous. Very dangerous. "You take the wheel first," said the policeman, "and take us as fast as you can, but don't forget what I taught you." Great advice, especially the negative, so my brain immediately forgot everything he taught me.

But I knew a little bit about setting goals, so I said to myself that I would exceed 115 mph. I knew my limits!

Off I went cruising at 70 mph. "Okay," said the policeman, "Let's take it up." And off I went, ,80…90…100 mph…110….118 mph. Was I thrilled? Safe, relieved, I slowed down and let my friend David have a go.

Within a minute he was doing 136 mph. I asked him afterwards how he managed it. David said that after I'd gone first, he could see himself going faster than me as it was now easier.

So stretch your goals – you'd be amazed as to what we are capable of. Ten years ago David Beckham was the only real master free-kick taker in the Premiership. He was so good they named a film after him *Bend it like Beckham*. Nowadays every team has one or two specialist free-kick takers

After Roger Bannister had broken the four-minute mile in May 1956, after years of training and dedication, within the same year, another thirty-seven people had done so. And the following year a whopping 300 people achieved the four-minute mile.

So stretch your goals just that little bit more. Instead of focussing around 115 mph, I should have targeted myself for 130. Just that little bit faster.

Observed Sales Calls

Structure

The process of observation and feedback can be summarised in this graphic:

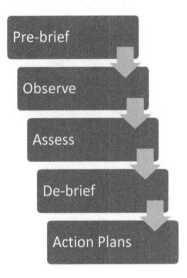

The Pre-brief

The purpose of the pre-brief is to set the scene for the accompanied interview. It is to assure the adviser that benefits will evolve from the meeting, and it is not an intention to find fault.

A good pre-brief will really set the scene between you and the adviser. Not only do you break the ice with the adviser but you prime the observation and you seek views from the adviser as to the areas he wants you to observe in particular - this is extremely useful when dealing with experienced individuals.

A suggested "agenda" of items to discuss in a pre-brief is as follows:

Suggested Pre-Brief Questions

- "I'd like to talk about your interview for ten minutes to give me a better handle on the client and to explore areas you want me to observe."

- "How was this client referred?"

- "What details have you got?"

- "What else do you know about them?"

- "What are you looking to achieve from the meeting?"

- "What's your aim?"

- "What is your client expecting from the meeting?"

- "What do they want from you?"

- "What did we agree at the last meeting?"

- "I'll be looking out for this..."

- "What areas do you want me to concentrate on?"

- "What would you like me to look out for?"

Observing a sales meeting

Our next step is to physically observe and objectively assess the meeting that has been carried out in front of us.

There are certain skills in observing and assessing the skills and knowledge of a salesperson. We'll concentrate today on observing and assessing a live meeting.

Introduce the coach

How were you introduced?

Be honest and upfront. If the client realises that this process is ultimately for their benefit, they'll see no problem in the meeting being observed.

Know what to look for

Remember the pre-brief points that you're looking out for. Recall the previous action points from previous meetings. Know the process of the sales meeting that you're observing.

Remember other interviews that you've observed to assist in the feedback.

Stay unobtrusive

Don't interrupt the meeting. Watch the adviser and the client, particularly non-verbal signals to assess the client's reaction.

Assess performance afterwards

Once the meeting has finished, spend a few minutes going through your notes to make some order of things. Summarise the good points to feedback and decide the areas that need focusing. Ensure you have all the evidence you need.

Do give the de-brief after the meeting - don't be tempted to sort it out the next morning, particularly if the meeting has occurred in the evening.

Don't Double the Talk

I was watching the halftime review of a major football match the other day. You know when the cameras zoom back to the studio and you have the pundits and experts giving you their opinion of the match?

Gary Lineker was doing his best to orchestrate the experts. Mark Lawrenson was chipping in with his words of wisdom about something, Alan Shearer had to give an angle on the same topic, and of course, Alan Hansen needed to convince the viewers that he was an expert with his own take on the same topic.

I thought, hold on, they're doing what sales managers do when accompanying their sales people on sales calls. Thankfully it's quite rare, but I've witnessed the salesperson making a point to the sales manager to prove he is the sales manager, gives another angle on the same point.

Doubling the talk, much to the frustration of the salesperson…and the sales manager.

So sales managers, don't chip in during the sales meeting. Your job is to coach afterwards, not add your penny's worth.

And Alan Hansen, we know you're an expert; you don't have to prove it to the viewer every time by repeating what Mark and Alan have already said. Alan, you're very experienced. It was almost twenty years ago you played for Liverpool, wasn't it…and you haven't managed a football team, have you? But you've been on BBC for years, haven't you, earning, I believe £1.5 million a year.

Bit naughty that, but I couldn't resist.

Your Best-Practice Playbook

I help to run a small village rugby team for thirteen-year-olds, and I'm part of a team of three coaches. This summer one of the coaches had a great idea. He asked us all to put on an email two or three plays or coaching drills or practice ideas that we'd used to help the boys play better rugby. As a result, we'd produced a playbook of dozens of useful drills, plays, and ways of improving the boys' rugby skills.

This season we're busy putting them into practice.

On holiday in France last year, our holiday rep produced a *Big Playbook of Great Days Out* with all contributions given by holiday makers during the summer. What a great initiative as every idea had been tried and tested.

• Do you have an active playbook in your sales team where all your salespeople and sales coaches contribute great ideas, best-practice tips, and techniques? You could have this as an online forum or wiki where everyone's encouraged to share and contribute.

• Or, as a team of coaches, do you have role play ideas, coaching techniques that you share somewhere?

• Or as sales managers, do you have a place where you share sales meeting content, motivational ideas, coaching tips, sales boosting ideas?

All successful modern teams pull together to share best practices. Remember, the whole is better than the sum of the individual parts.

Giving Feedback – The De-brief

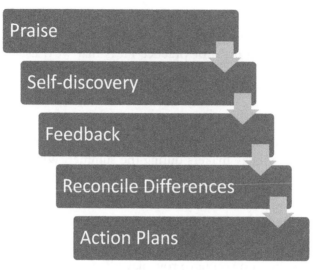

Encourage self-assessment

This allows the coach to establish the adviser's recollection of events and some reasons behind them. Self-assessment also gives the coach something to build their own feedback on, particularly if the adviser recognises some negative points.

The whole emphasis of coaching is the need for self-discovery - allowing the experienced adviser to re-think the interview and perhaps improve their performance. Why is self-discovery so important? Here are three reasons for you:

- Prevents feeling of dependency by the adviser on the coach. This can arise when the coach always takes the lead in suggesting ideas, options, and alternatives. Creates self - dependency.

- Creates feeling of being able to satisfy all problems themselves. This ownership will ensure they use their new skill or alternative method.

- Creates feeling of satisfaction if they were able to generate the ideas or alternatives. "You really know this job."

Provide observations

The coach should now state what they observed. Be specific and refer to actual evidence that you wrote down. Keep to the actions of the person and not the person themselves. Commenting on the person can create a negative attitude. For example:

"You decided to say this…"

Commenting on the action could produce this:

"This sentence allowed the client to react in this way."

Reconcile differences.

Don't get into an argument. Seek their views.

Agree on the next step

They should be encouraged to identify potential solutions and possibly development needs.

Once you've agreed to a goal or an improvement area for the adviser, you could latch onto the GROW model to allow them to see through some actions to do something about it. Self-discovery is essential with experienced people.

Nine steps to coach live telephone or video sales calls

1. Sell the session
2. Have a structure
3. Are they an "A" grade student
4. Give dollops of praise
5. Rather better than "you have a good voice"
6. Look away
7. Use "different" not "wrong"
8. Give sandwich feedback
9. Work with priorities

Sell the session

Far too many inside salespeople have been coached before with the sole intention of having their style observed and compared against a checklist of what good looks like; it's not coaching and shouldn't be called it. Use words such as:

"Now before we start, let me show you how this coaching is going to be different and valuable for you. I'm able to work with you now by listening in to your calls and giving you expert feedback on what you are doing really well and suggest possible areas that you can do differently to make you even better. I'm not going to checklist you and mark you, that's so not what this is all about – I'm here to work with you and make you even better than you are right now."

Have a structure

Structure is imperative to inside salespeople, and the tip I want to give you here is to outline this for them at the outset and continue to signpost it throughout the coaching session. Signposting is a key ingredient for them when dealing with salespersons on the phone, so we need to signpost them during the coaching session. Remember, no surprises.

"After our initial chat we'll listen to two calls without stopping, then I'd like you to break off for a moment whilst we have some feedback. Then we can go back on a call, and if you could break off after each one we'll have a brief feedback before going on to the next call. In about forty-five minutes we'll then wrap up and take your thoughts. Sound okay?"

Are they an "A" grade student?

I call this a pre-brief. Before the first call comes in, set the scene by asking them what they would want you to specifically listen for and give them feedback on. This often comes as a surprise to them as previous coaching involves going straight into a call. So be prepared to probe on this area as you'll get the "I dunno" answer. Relate it to some training that might have occurred beforehand or maybe to some form of feedback.

Do you remember at school when you turned in your homework and received the results? Did you constantly get A's or were you more of a B student or C possibly – with the note from teacher saying "room for improvement"?

Kind of brings back a memory, doesn't it, but this can be extremely useful when pre-briefing. If you get little information from them after asking the question, it's worth asking them to grade their ability in handling calls. You could use the B+ format or marks out of ten – it doesn't matter.

"So if you were to grade your average call from 1 to 10, where would you place yourself?"

"Urrr, I guess 7 or 8."

"That's great. Out of interest, what would a 10-out-of-10 call look like?"

"For you to get a perfect 10, what would you want to do differently?"

This works so it's worth giving it a go.

Give dollops of praise

This morning my car was covered in ice so I popped out ten minutes early to run the engine and de-ice and de-mist it. I ran the engine for about five minutes so when I climbed in, the car was lovely and toasty and the engine humming, unlike me!

Just like a car on a very frosty morning, my salespeople needed warming up, too, and the best way I've found to do this is to listen to one or two calls to start with and point out to them the positive aspects that I noticed. I've found the most effective way to do this is to say what you heard them do or say. Explain why this is good and the positive impact it had on the salesperson. For example:

"I really do like the way your voice sounds chirpy and enthusiastic. You're able to do this because you have a good vocal range and can stretch your voice to maximum effect. The salesperson feels as though you are very human and genuinely interested in them. Well done."

Rather better than, *"You have a good voice."*

Even the most hardened and experienced salesperson will revel in this, and it is particularly important for the newer seller who is often a little nervous. The next call you listen to will be far more natural and an indication as to how they normally work.

Look away

Once I'm hooked up with the phone listening device, I like to look away from the salesperson and their computer screen as you can easily get caught up in the detail of the call and irrelevant observations.

It's the verbal and vocal aspects we want to pick up on. I want to listen to the voices of both people; I want to sense the salesperson and how they are feeling. How do they react to what's being said, their tone of voice, their pace? That way I can look for matching and leading, and emotions rather than the content and subject of the call.

Use "different" not "wrong"

This is so simple yet so powerful. I've overheard many coaches giving feedback focussed on what the person is doing wrong. Now this is fine as making the person aware of this is a major purpose of the coaching session. I prefer to be more practical and suggest something they should do differently which overcomes the weak area.

This is much more motivational and practical.

For example, if they are talking too fast and the salesperson can't understand them I would say something like:

"I noticed the salesperson asked you to repeat what you were saying a couple of times. Something you could do differently is to add a bit more of a gap between your sentences. If you were to do this, the salesperson would understand your question the first time, and this would save you time."

Rather than, *"I noticed the salesperson asked you to repeat what you were saying. This is because you were speaking too quickly."*

Give sandwich feedback

It's as old as "them thar hills", sometimes called burger feedback aka the McDonald's model or just sandwich feedback. The one that works for me is this:

1. Tell them what they did well and the impact. Be genuine.
2. Here's what you could do differently and the impact it would have. Just one thing, and it must be the priority
3. Your overall impression of the call, which needs to be positive and upbeat.

It's three parts and can be done quickly and efficiently. Don't get into longwinded discussion; if they don't agree with you, that's just fine. Get over it and move on, and next time give some evidence as to why doing it differently would make a difference.

Work with priorities

The longest time you'll want to work with someone is one hour – I normally work for about forty-five minutes. This gives you time to listen to plenty of calls and give feedback.

However, we can't cover every aspect and give lots of varying feedback. Not only would this be nigh on impossible in the timeframe but frankly quite de-motivating if there are just too many points discussed.

So instead, focus on just one or two main priority points of feedback that you can spot early on. Priority points, once taken care of, have a knock-on effect on other areas, and it's this feedback we want to give. Then give them a chance to change on the next call and feel the difference it makes and then to try this new angle a few times during your coaching. Not only is this good training practice, i.e. repetition is the mother of all skill, but it's very motivating when you've given some feedback and they've adopted it and are getting better results.

The Italian Job and Hindsight

One of my favourite of all films is *The Italian Job* starring Michael Caine and the 1960s Mini Cooper. Last week I was watching it for the thirty-second time, this time on glorious HD and relishing the final scene when the gold was about to slip away forever over the cliff as the coach dangled precariously over the edge.

Later that night I logged onto a Michael Caine *Italian Job* Internet forum where the discussion heading was, "What would you do now, to rescue the gold?"

People were putting all sorts of ideas up online, from emptying the fuel tank to lassoing the gold with a rope. And some pretty good ideas too.

This made me think again on the power of hindsight where we are all very much wiser. Hindsight is remarkable, and as coaches, is one of our most powerful tools. Never be wary of asking your salesperson coachee to revisit the sale or the meeting and ask themselves, with the power of hindsight, how they would do it differently.

Just change the way you ask this question, otherwise you'll get very predictable. I have an old remote control device in my case which I bring out, and physically rewind my coachee without saying a word, as a different way of introducing the hindsight question.

It always works.

Personally if I were Michael Caine, I would let the gold fall out of the back of the coach, quickly drive away, hiding the evidence of the collision. Then I'd go get the gold later. Do you have any better ideas?

Beware the defensive walls

I'm travelling through South Wales on a train at the moment, and I've been looking at the many castles that sprinkle the countryside here. Built to withstand the cannon blasts and explosions of attacking armies, many are still in pristine condition.

People also have alarmingly strong defensive walls, and this is no more apparent than when coaching people in a high-pressure sales environment. This is where performance coaching really works.

The coach has just got to get to the point. I observe many coaches who skirt around the issue, dangle leading questions at the salesperson, and play games. Salespeople see through this and put up their thick concrete walls, and no benefit will come from the coaching session. You see, salespeople bristle with emotions and beliefs about their performance. It goes with the trade.

Say what you see and invite a comment: What could they do differently? Don't accuse of low performance. Get to the point, help them be aware of how they are performing, and allow them to see the way forward, not you. That is the key. As soon as you see a trace of the defensive wall going up, examine how you're making them feel and get to the point.

Just passing the Millennium Stadium in Cardiff. Now that's a fortress modelled on Welsh castles. No wonder the Welsh are so good at rugby.

Ten golden dual sales call rules

Essentially coaching involves very personal styles, and seasoned coaches are unique in their approach. However, there are ten principles to remember.

1. Taking over the call - when dual calling with salespeople the urge can be strong to take over the call, particularly with newer recruits. Don't!

2. Loss of order versus training need - a very difficult decision. How do you balance losing the sale by not stepping in versus the patience to allow a self-discovered learning need?

3. Tell versus ask style – one of the oldest discussion points in the history of coaching.

4. Help to learn – do you teach people or allow them to learn by providing encouragement?

5. Experienced versus new recruits - knowing how to treat people differently is a great skill in coaching. Experience deserves more empowerment.

6. Focus on one or two areas – priorities bring results. Remember Pareto's famous 80:20 rule. It survives in all aspects of life. Eighty percent of the pub's business comes from twenty percent of its salespersons. Eighty percent of business comes from twenty percent of your coachee client bank. Eighty percent of your income comes from twenty percent of your people. In this instance eighty percent of improvement in performance

comes from twenty percent of those potential improvements. The trick is finding the twenty percent priority.

7. Coach before the call – help your coachee to consider areas of potential improvements he/she would like coaching on after the observation. This way you work on the priority.

8. Regard your coaching day as a learning day – this means eliminating targets for the day so you focus purely of learning and development issues.

9. Need a selling model - a good coach needs a process model to follow. You've got to compare against something, and even the best salesperson/coach needs a crutch.

10. What do you take forward? – how much coaching is forgotten about in the hustle and bustle of business life because it wasn't taken forward by all concerned? The coach is in an ideal position to take the coaching forward.

Feedback is like engine oil

My car is serviced a couple of times a year, and I'm amazed at the price and complexity of the oil it receives. Synthetic, non-synthetic, generic...all sorts of names.

But the point is that my car guzzles the right kind of oil; it has the right qualities for the engine I drive; it has just enough quantity; and it's also timely, changed at a certain mileage interval determined by very bright engineers.

I like to think the same is true for feedback to your salespeople when you're coaching. Giving feedback is essential at all times as it keeps salespeople at the top of their game, and salespeople have to be there all the time.

So does your feedback have those three qualities – quality, quantity, and timeliness? Do you offer just one item each time you offer feedback? The most important, the priority, the number one?

Do you provide the right quality of feedback?

And finally, do you deliver it with timeliness? It's totally pointless giving feedback long after the moment. We've forgotten the moment, can't relate the feedback instantly, and the salesperson won't be able to comment and apply it because the moment has gone.

But really, £100 to replace an oil sump, that's ridiculous, but I guess, you get what you pay for, and feedback is invaluable.

The SPAM on the job feedback model

As a child, I had one really big decision every morning. It was to decide what filling to place in between my two slices of Farmer's Wife white bread for my lunch. The dilemma was Spam meat from the tin or sandwich spread from the jar? Invariable the verdict was Spam. Easy to slice, would last forever, and oddly enough, rather tasty.

SPAM is a way of structuring your feedback with your team members when you're carrying out *on-the-job* coaching. As an energetic and active coach, you wander your workplace, listen to calls, observe salesperson engagement, and help your team to sell more and give superior salesperson service.

Salesperson engagement coaching doesn't happen behind closed doors. Believe me, it doesn't.

Here's how SPAM works. You happen to sit down on the counter and observe one of your teams advising on a product with a salesperson, maybe a credit card or bespoke insurance package.

You observe them, and in your mind, you're comparing them with some best-practice techniques. As the sales manager, you know what good looks like, if you don't refer to your team's best-practice playbook. You don't have a best-practice playbook? It's all in your head?

That's dangerous if you ever leave.

So the engagement has ended. In order to give them the benefit of your wisdom and best practice, you want to give them feedback. Now slice up your SPAM.

S stands for self-discovery. Classic. Ask them how they did, what went well in their opinion, if they could do it again, how might they tweak it. Now we know the outcome, i.e. the salesperson's reaction, what might you change?

P is for a positive piece of feedback. Let them know specifically and in detail what you particularly admired about the observation. Make it real, not that your shoes were shiny or the colour of your tie was stunning. Find something that was the best aspect of the engagement, the one of many. Remember, children need eleven positives to outweigh a negative, and adults, although a little more robust, still need five positives to one negative.

A is alternative. Next, launch straight into a suggestion from you on how you can do it differently, an idea on some aspect of the engagement, something very specific that will make the meeting even better. Don't debate, just move onto the…

M, which stands for a meaningful overall impression. Remember, primacy and recency. People remember the beginning and end of any conversation, so end on a high, an overall good first impression. "Fabulous meeting with Mrs. Brown. That lady has an excellent impression now of our company, thanks to you, Mary, well-done."

As Dale Carnegie said, "*Salespeople bristle with emotions.*" I say don't ruffle them. Make them feel good but help them to get even better.

And then leave, as I had to do since my long-winded decision as to sandwich spread or Spam usually meant I was late for school. Oh, and does anyone else pine over Unigate's Farmer's Wife sliced white bread adorned with sandwich spread? Totally lush.

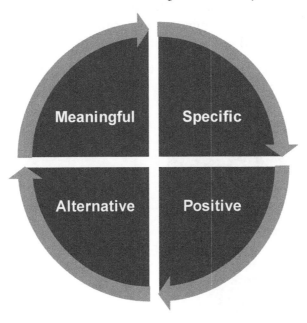

PAMing, not SPAMing

Sounds rather painful, doesn't it? And believe me, for the person you're coaching, it really is agonizing.

So if you're just PAMing, then you're missing out on the most valuable and rewarding piece. Be genuine and curious with the S. Ask in different ways. A favourite of mine is to ask them to imagine they have a Sky TV remote control device and press rewind to do it again, what would they do differently. Or imagine a time machine and whiz back ten minutes in time. On occasion, I've taken my watch off and physically rewound the clock ten minutes, once I jumped up and adjusted the clock on the wall to make my point.

After a few times of encouraging self-discovery, you don't need to say anything. Just go silent and look at them – they'll soon fill the silence with their self-discovery.

Self-discovery builds long-term improvement because it motivates people to become self-sufficient in improving their performance, which is the ultimate goal of any coach…isn't it?

So make sure you SPAM, not PAM, and you'll help your salesperson to self-improve their own performance and make your life so much easier.

McDonald's burger and fries feedback

"Can you organise the tea for the children" were the last words my wife uttered as she headed to the car and the post-Christmas sales. And the last thing I wanted to do was cook, so we jumped into my car and within ten minutes were sitting down in an iconic eatery of the twenty-first century – McDonald's.

Tucking into our burger, fries, and milkshake reminded me of giving feedback following an observation at work. The memory of burgers, fries, and shake can help you structure your feedback.

Let me explain

You see, I always start by eating the fries. They get cold very quickly, and eating cold fries is not enjoyable. So I tuck into these straightaway. Occasionally they satisfy my appetite on their own, but rarely.

Then I gorge on my Big Mac, enjoying the taste and benefitting from the nutrients. Yes, there are plenty in the Big Mac.

Finally, I slurp back the milkshake because this takes a while to thin out so the shake can crawl through the narrow straw. Drinking this too early is impossible until it thaws a little.

And finally, when I leave the restaurant, I make an action plan to diet immediately.

So how does this relate to giving feedback to someone on your team who has just performed something and you've been observing their performance? Well...

Firstly, you ask them genuinely how they got on, what worked well, what didn't, and what to do differently if they could do it again. Just like my fries, the time to do this is immediately, and in the same way as my fries, the impact will wear with time. You have to ask these questions right at the beginning.

Then you evolve to your feedback, taking the components of the burger. The bread is a filler – here you offer something that worked really well that you observed, and the more specific the better. Then comes the development feedback, the meat patty. Here you suggest something that they can do differently next time, not what they did wrong, but a suggestion for improvement. This is the most beneficial part.

The milkshake comes next, where you polish the feedback off with a big picture comment on how effectively they performed. An overall favourable, lasting impression.

And finally, the exit through the door, the action plan. What are they going to take from your coaching session to their next meeting or performance?

Uncanny, isn't it, how giving live feedback after an observation is so closely related to a McDonald's Big Mac, fries, and shake. The only difference is that we can give lots of feedback to develop our people, but we ought not to eat too many McDonald's meals.

So remember:

- Fries – self-discovery questions
- Bread – piece of positive feedback
- Meat patty – what they can do differently
- Milkshake – overall good impression

Did you know McDonald's now publishes the calorie content of their meals, and mine added up to a portly 1,470 calories; perhaps I need some feedback about my holiday eating habits. I must start my diet now.

Let's build strengths

I was very fortunate to speak in my tenth country since I began my own speaking and training business – Bangladesh.

Each country provides me with a different perspective and understanding of a culture that I haven't experienced. Bangladesh was no exception – Bangladeshis are a unique people.

Amongst their manner was the need to compliment others rather than criticise. Indeed the habit of "saving face" predominates in the Far East. Instead of giving feedback on weaknesses, they make a big show of someone's strengths. As a result, people's confidence grows, and this helps to move everyone forward in the right manner.

I like this.

So next time we're coaching and wanting to give your salesperson some feedback, let's build strengths and let them prevail. This will empower and give them confidence to do more of the same. The growing strengths will outweigh any weaknesses.

After all, it's much more fun showing our strengths than trying to eliminate weaknesses.

And did you know that ninety-five percent of Indian restaurants in the UK are, in fact, Bangladeshi? I didn't.

Why do we focus on what's wrong all the time?

I was watching the halftime report from the Test Rugby when England was playing New Zealand. The pundits kept criticizing the players from both sides.

Later that day, Match of the Day and Alan Hansen were doing the same.

My daughter's school report came through, highlighting her weaknesses, and the teacher, during the open evening, kept banging on about Bethan's shortcomings so she could improve, with only a minor mention of her many strengths.

And when I was observing a sales manager giving feedback to one of his salespeople last week, the big focus was on improving the flaws.

Why, oh, why can't we put more emphasis on our strengths, our plus points, our assets?

That way we could boost these even more so that our weaknesses become tiny in comparison.

So sales managers out there, try just giving praise, point out the strengths, and see what they can do to build on these alone.

Let the strengths prevail. After all, for most of us, me included, I have weaknesses, and there's precious little I can do about changing them. They're with me for life. Accept it.

The Sales One-to-One

Don't let 'em wallow in slump

One of my favourite haunts is the Red Lion Pub just off the River Severn, but to get there by foot you have to walk the water meadows. The dogs make it across in any weather. So do I, but when it's really wet and muddy you can easily get your Wellington boots stuck in the mud, and it's a nightmare to get out of the quicksand-like texture. Your salespeople are the same when stuck in their mud, or their sales slump. Don't let them wallow in it. Help them to climb out safely and perform once again. Here's how.

Spot

Spot them when they're in a slump. Metrics and KPIs hastened by some sort of exception report or sales dashboard can help, but regular communication and one-to-ones with your team will soon show you they're in a slump.

FISH for the cause

Use the FISH technique to help them figure out the problem, and more importantly, the cause of their slump. FISH is to focus on the problem, identify the cause, solve it, and then work out how to do it long-term. Work out a plan with them and put the plan into action.

Empathy

Show empathy with them. Don't sympathise but understand where they are and how to get out of it. Guide, direct, and encourage.

Support them

Provide training, observation of best practice. Do lots of coaching with them, and if you're in a call centre, do live and recorded call coaching. Do some mild counselling, if this is appropriate. Be there with them. Make more contact but don't micro-manage. Keep an eye.

KPIs

Monitor them carefully and try to get some quick victories and reward these. Lots of quick, small wins are more beneficial for motivation than waiting for a large win. Reward effort and process rather than just successes.

These steps will help your seller get out of their slump, and they'll be rewarded with continuous success. Just like me on the water meadows as I'm rewarded with a cold glass of Old Rosie Cider at the Red Lion Inn.

Six Salespeople a-Slumping

When Christmas approaches, we like to sing "12 Days of Christmas", so I've included a new verse – the six salespeople a-slumping. I've six different salespeople and the character behind the slump. These six really do represent the main types of salesperson a-slumping, and you can use them to recognise your people and more importantly, how you can help them come out of the slump.

Concerned Connor

Easy to spot because they look very worried and concerned about their slump. They'll probably come to you for help before you can arrange it. They're very cooperative with you, put up no resistance, and genuinely want to work with you to get out of their slump.

FISH them, guide them, give them more ideas to help their slump and pull them out. Regular coaching and feedback of live and recorded calls would be most welcomed by Concerned Connor.

Indifferent Ian

Ian is in denial. He won't recognise or admit he's in a slump. It's just a glitch, a temporary setback, or he might just have given up worrying about it, preferring to ignore the slump altogether and maybe it'll go away.

With Ian, you need to do the Alcoholics Anonymous trick of getting him to realise he's in a slump before you can figure out the cause and address it. Be prepared for a lengthy battle.

Care as it may be stress-induced.

Fearful Freddie

Poor old Freddie is paralysed with fear. They're so concerned about the consequences of a slump, they lose all ability to get out of it and fear the worst. It's an Inner Game thing from now on. They're capable but their mind's not in it, so you need to do some confidence work with them, turning negative thoughts into positive thoughts. Tame their inner demon, their gremlin, who is sitting on their shoulder telling them they're useless, not cut out for selling, and should've stayed in their nine-to-five admin role.

Once their confidence and self-esteem are back, coach them. FISH for cause, work out a plan, and guide them to successful performance again.

Hostile Harry

Angry, hostile, and blaming everyone but himself for his downturn. It's the leads; it's the product; we're too expensive.

Even worse, you might have a passive-aggressive, quietly blaming and undermining everyone else.

Check the hygiene factors – company policy, salary, management style – yes, you – working conditions. See if any of these are irritating him. Control Harry. FISH him to realise there might be a problem, and the cause could relate to his activities.

Only then can you direct him, coach him, and bring his performance back to where it should be.

Remember, though, that Harry is contagious. His attitude might infect your other salespeople, particularly if they're in close proximity, such as a call centre. Treat him quickly and consider whether you really want him on your team.

Unmotivated Umran

Umran is unmotivated, lacking in zest, has moved to a helplessness motivational zone. Check him for hygiene factors and then focus on building his confidence and self-esteem. Get some zest back into him, return his mojo, then FISH for cause and build his performance.

Stressed Scotty

Stress could be the reason for his downturn. Or his downturn may have caused his stress. You can recognise stress in salespeople in three ways. One, they've changed, gone all quiet on you. Two, they fly off the handle at the slightest provocation. Three, they've just given up.

Don't be a hero. If you're not good at counselling stress, hire someone who is. Get HR involved if you suspect stress, but deal with it.

So there we have six salespeople a-slumping for you to use to recognise if any of your people are in a slump and some tips and ideas to help you get them out and back to peak performance. And roll on Christmas, that's what I say.

Six Salespeople a-Slumping, five Golden Rings, four Calling Birds, three French Hens, two Turtle Doves, and a Partridge in a Pear Tree.

The science of the sales one-to-one

Below is the flowchart with all the tools that you need to run a performance-based one-to-one with your salespeople. One-to-ones normally occur monthly in most inside sales-led businesses, but they can be run more often if desired and the situation requires.

Remember, the aim of the one-to-one is to move the consultant forward in some way, to create some agreed actions that increase or maintain performance levels.

It's not a form-filling exercise, although if I had a pound for every form-filling one-to-one I've seen...here's the science.

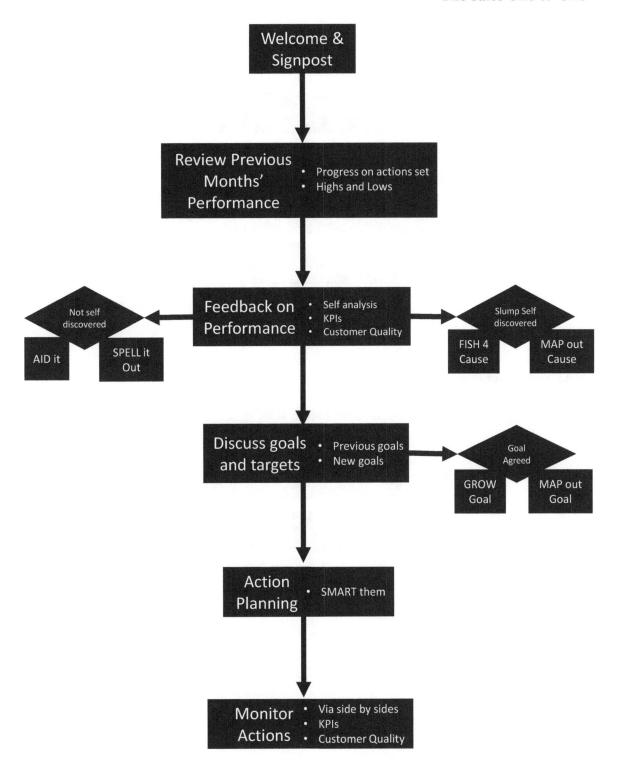

Here are the tools:

SPELL it out

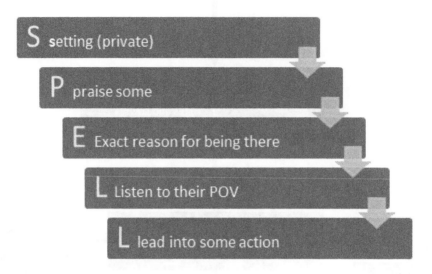

MAP your listening

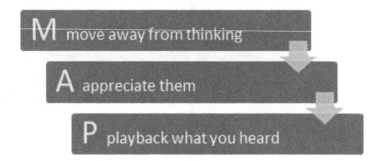

AID the feedback

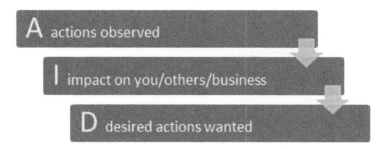

FISH the cause

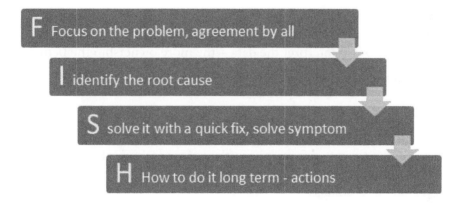

The art of one-to-ones

This is the negotiable part of the one-to-one, the area where skills and techniques comes in, where your personality abounds and your experience and tactics help you to arrive at some generative action with your salesperson.

Let's see how this reveals itself.

Welcome and signpost

Usual ice-breaking works here, but don't drag on the analysis of the penalty in last night's match. In fact, if you've asked your salesperson to prepare the one-to-one, you can progress very smoothly. After all, time is important and good one-to-ones last around forty-five minutes.

Ask them to think about their highs and lows for the previous period. Share your sales dashboard with them so they can judge their own KPIs and other quality scores. It's a good idea to train them on how to interpret the data – the more ownership the better.

Get down to business quickly; after all, this is coaching.

Review previous performance

Open up to your salesperson immediately. Go for self-discovery and ownership straight off the bat. Ask them about their performance in the past month, the highs and lows. Ask them how they've been getting on with the agreed actions from the last one-to-one. Allow them to talk; don't dominate proceedings.

Feedback on performance

Let there be praise. Immersed in the hubbub of a busy sales organisation with a number of salespeople to manage, quotas to achieve and pressure from all sides…we forget that salespeople need praise.

And lots of it too.

On average, children need nine positives to outweigh any one negative. I know this from firsthand experience coaching young boys in rugby from the ages of six to thirteen. We used the technique of only building strengths. Lucky for us, Rugby Union has a position for any lad, however small, short, fast, slow, lumbering they were. We never criticised or fed back what they weren't doing, just positives. And it worked.

The best feedback is self-discovered by your salesperson. We know this.

Self-discovered feedback can be facilitated by helping them to understand the KPIs and the other measures on your sales dashboard. At least they can admit to a fall in performance or a slip or two.

If they haven't realised it, then you need to provide feedback. Feedback is essential because they don't know what they don't know. Here's how.

Remember at least five pieces of praise, then use the tool – AID.

- Actions – what are they doing not so well?

- Impact – what's the effect of this, to the business, salespersons, themselves?

- Desired – what is it we want differently?

AID works really well to provide punchy feedback to arrive at a goal or new objective. It won't solve the performance slump. You need FISH for that. This is the science.

But what if the salesperson doesn't run with the feedback or disagrees with it? Maybe you know you have a battle on your hands as they're quite feisty and are prone to push back and use defensiveness. This happens more than we like to admit.

SPELL it out

Use SPELL. Or spell it out to them.

- Setting – best in private

- Praise – lots of praise. If you can, even past praise can work.

- Exact – outline the exact reason you're having the conversation.

- Listen – hear their point of view and don't interrupt.

- Lead – lead them into an action plan.

Identify the cause

So there we have the problem agreed and focused on. Next we identify the cause of the slump, the root cause. Many coaches and sales managers will try to identify the symptoms of the slump and solve these. That's not good enough.

For example a salesperson might be slumping. Her numbers are down. Her motivation has suffered, so the sales manager tries to re-motivate her with some challenges and new targets. Believe me, I've seen this.

The symptom is being treated not the cause.

We passed through Calais on our return from holiday in France on the last Saturday in August. I was fully expecting the port to be busy, some queuing involved, but I was taken aback by the five-hour queue outside the port. The tailbacks were caused by the migrants trying to board every lorry, truck, and RV heading for the UK.

The migrants, from Somalia, Sudan, Ethiopia, just wanted simply to live in the UK, which they believe is a sanctuary and a place where they can have a better life.

And they were doing all sorts of antics to get on the ferry, causing traffic carnage in Calais.

The symptom was traffic and illegal boarding of the trucks heading for the UK, so the authorities erected twelve-foot-high fences around the port, drafted in hundreds of police armed with rubber bullets and riot gear, and tried to refrain the migrants from boarding the ferries.

However, this wasn't solving the root cause.

The root cause was the reason they fled their home countries. War-torn, torture, lack of food and shelter—whatever the reason, that was why they fled their homes in the first place.

So we need to drill down to the root cause for our salesperson's slump.

When they're talking it's a good idea to utilise the MAP listening technique. That way they can spill it all out.

And then you can fix it and develop an action plan to solve it over the long-term.

Discuss goals and targets

Now we have some goals to achieve either arrived at as a result of FISHing, SPELLing, or AIDing.

Once the salesperson has a goal or an objective they want to achieve, then it's a straightforward matter of using GROW to arrive at an action plan or two.

In the Will section of GROW when you're discussing what their plan of action is going to be, we need to be disciplined to ensure that the actions decided are SMART.

Is the action specific enough? Is it measurable? – what gets measured gets done – is it achievable with their current capability? Is it relevant to their role, and will it work, and finally, is there some sort of timescale attached to it? Otherwise it'll just run on forever.

Monitor Actions

With the one-to-one over for another month, it's very easy to get bogged down in the detail of a busy contact centre and forget what was agreed until next month.

This is a mistake.

The actions need to be monitored by you. Maybe a weekly catch-up is needed. Carry out your "on-the-job" coaching and observations. Keep an eye on the relevant KPI. If you SMARTened the plans in the first place, you'll have measures to watch out for.

FISHing a Sales Slump

There's an old saying. Give a man a fish and you feed him for a day; teach him to fish and you lose him for the whole weekend.

Seriously, fishing is the most popular sport in the UK, carried out by millions of men, and it's also a very useful coaching tool to help get to the cause of a problem.

The problem I want to explore here is the low performance of a salesperson—a poor performer, someone who is not achieving their sales targets or metrics.

The answer to resolving their poor performance is to do something different to help them. But we shouldn't even attempt intervening until we know what's causing the downturn in performance. FISH can help you coach your seller to reveal the issues.

Let me explain how.

Just like all good alcoholics, they have to recognise there's a problem before conquering their addiction. Likewise a poor performer must realise that there's a problem. It's not a blip or just temporary; there is an issue and we need to sort this out.

The F – focusing on the problem will allow you, the coach, to ask questions to help them realise what the problem is. Produce metrics, trends, exception reports, evidence if you need to, but your seller has to realise themselves what the problem is first.

Next is the reason for the sales slump. The cause. Ask questions to find out what's caused the slump. Don't impose your own thoughts on the cause. They have to see it. That's the I – identify the cause.

S is for solving it...quickly. This may not be possible, of course; it may require a long, drawn-out solution over months involving training, coaching, motivation, prospecting, or whatever. But what we want here are some early victories, some quick wins to patch things over.

H is for how to move forward long-term. What's the master plan? What's the goal or series of goals we need to achieve? Get your GROW out at this point and start GROWing their new goals to help them get out of their sales slump...and perhaps take up fishing. Millions of others have.

Give a man a fish and you feed him for the day...teach him to fish and you lose him for the whole weekend.

Demonstrating Sales Skills

Breathing your own exhaust

Deep in the bowels of the ferry. That's where we were directed on our journey to our French holiday. The English Channel was above us as we were below the water line. Over a hundred cars all spewing their exhaust in a confined area. I was reluctant to breathe because of the intoxicating, secondhand air.

What about you in your business or your career?

Are you breathing your own exhaust?

Are you mixing with the same people, doing everything in-house, working with the same teams year in year out? If so, you're probably devoid of new, refreshing ideas.

I know of companies I work for who are proud of their long-serving employees. Some of them have been there for over thirty years. This may have advantages, but I think, in the modern economy, the strengths outweigh the weaknesses as ideas from outside, fresh-thinking, new angles are hard to come by from the same people.

Do you mix outside of your cocoon? Do you attend industry seminars, network with others, attend Mastermind groups? Do you alter your association affiliations from time to time? I've seen people who belong to the same trade association year after year who also become stale for new ideas.

Do you bring in new people? Yes, advertise internally because that's the right thing, but encourage others to come into your business.

If you do, you'll be like me when I managed to crawl out of the bowels of that ferry and into the fresh air of the cabins and outside areas. Breathing the new air, I was able to have new momentum and perspectives as I headed to the duty-free area.

How to demonstrate sales skills - MEDIC

Occasionally you stumble across something really clever that you find yourself using time and time again. Early in my career I came across MEDIC, a really simple but ever-so-clever acronym that just makes every training session you ever deliver bring results.

MEDIC can be used when you're putting together a session with only a few minutes' preparation, so it's great with one-to-one training or "Sitting with Nellie"-type training.

Use the system and your sessions will be well-structured and work. MEDIC is an acronym which stands for:

- Motivate

- Explain

- Demonstrate

- Imitate

- Coach

Motivate

Never forget that people who are learning something need to see the benefits of doing so. We live in a WIIFM world – what's in it for me? I firmly believe that all trainers should also be salespeople at heart and always be willing and able to sell their training to anyone who cares to ask. It's so dangerous to assume everyone wants to be there on the course or to be at the receiving end of a training session. Many don't, and with today's choices, people can move on somewhere else if they wish.

We simply have to give some benefits to them of learning what we are going to teach them. That's why I made a point of giving you some benefits at the beginning of this article.

Let me give you an example of MEDIC in action which I used just the other day with my eleven-year-old son Lewis. Now Lewis just loves boiled eggs, and he really loves mine. Now I can't cook anything else, I'm afraid, just boiled eggs, but I do cook a vastly superior boiled egg.

I thought it was time to teach my son how to do it. Sort of like passing skills on from father to son! I motivated him with a couple of benefits.

"Lewis, if you learn to boil an egg, this means that you can enjoy a perfect boiled egg whenever you wish. Also, the method I'll teach you will ensure you have that perfect, soft yolk that you love so much."

Explain

Whatever you're teaching will probably need some explanation. Sometimes we're teaching something that's quite technical, such as the laws relating to selling mortgages, or the process of overcoming objections in selling. So there needs to be some explaining. This is what we call in the business "chalk and talk" usually accompanied by a flipchart. Here are some tips to help your explanation:

- Explain in a logical sequence

- Ensure you're clear and concise

- Don't rush

- Use small easily digestible chunks

- Avoid jargon

- Use questions to test understanding

- Using visual aids to aid understanding

- Use anecdotes, acronyms, stories - anything to make remembering easier.

- Make it interesting

With the explanation, please get them to do it rather than you, especially if you are training a group of people. This is the cornerstone of accelerated learning – get them to do it. Set up an activity so they read up on the explanation and explain to each other. Give them a case study so they discover it themselves. Run a group discussion so the learned ones educate the non-learned ones. Allow a bit of trial and error. Run a group brainstorm to see how much they do know.

With my boiled eggs with Lewis, I broke down the explanation into four key steps and explained each one separately.

- Step 1 is to boil the water.

- Step 2 is to lower the egg into the water.

- Step 3 is to time for four minutes exactly.

- Step 4 (might I say the true secret, so don't tell anyone) is to remove the pan and pour cold water into the pan, displacing the hot water. That way you stop the egg cooking.

Demonstration

Next comes the demonstration. Skills or processes or anything that involves doing something or saying something can be demonstrated. You, as the trainer, could do this. Or you could get someone else in to do it – maybe an expert, since you can't be an expert at everything. You could use a DVD or a media clip on your laptop.

Whoever does it is not the issue – it's how it's done. Here are some tips:

- Keep the demo visible

- Demo in small stages

- Use real equipment, forms, etc.

- Demo at an appropriate speed. Slower at first is best

- Explain as you go

- Allow time for questions

- And before you even start, do make sure you've practised

Because I'd broken down my boiled egg steps into four stages, I was able to demonstrate each step to Lewis.

Imitation

Next comes the imitation. In training this is so important, and unfortunately, the bit often missed out when time gets tight – and it always does.

When people practise something they start to get things "in the muscle". It becomes second nature.

When I pull away at a junction in my car, yes, I move up the gears; but I don't recall doing it. I just do it instinctively – it's in my "muscle memory"

Role play is a typical imitation activity, or a case study, pictograms, cartooning, debates, group discussion, crosswords, a quiz, a test, a game. The list goes on.

Or you could just ask them to perform the skill in front of you to see that they can do it.

Coach

Whilst they're performing, that's when coaching comes in. Now coaching is a subject of many more articles. Suffice it to say that the art of coaching is to watch them, pause them and ask how they're doing so far, what's going well, what's not going so well, what could they do differently. Only if necessary do you tell them where they've gone wrong.

It's very emotional learning something new. Inside us we feel threat and intimidation. When we don't know how to do something we get nervous, so go easy on the feedback. Imagine the delegate was you learning the skill. It's not easy. Encouragement gets more results than criticism.

Occasionally you'll want to get your learner to loop back to explain or demonstrate bit again, maybe if they missed something, so be gracious to do this.

So there we have MEDIC – motivate, explain, demonstrate, imitate, and coach. Follow the steps whenever you put a training session together and you won't go far wrong.

As for Lewis and the boiled eggs, we got to the imitation stage and my wife walked in and interrupted the show. Claire said that Lewis is too young to boil water. She probably has a point.

I'm now grounded for a week!

How to explain for maximum understanding

We all have to present information or an idea or a proposal, and we aim to achieve maximum understanding of our message.

My holiday to France this year is always a challenge when it comes to speaking to the French shopkeeper or passer-by. My French is basic zero-level stuff and my accent is non-existent, so I have to revert to other methods to get my message across. Sign language, using pictures or drawings, lots of smiles, sometimes slower, louder.

Here's twenty ways you can get your message across more effectively:

1. An analogy
2. A prop or an object to illustrate
3. An example
4. A quote
5. Some stats
6. A joke
7. A story or metaphor
8. A visual aid such as a diagram
9. A sound bite, song, or tune
10. Summarising and repeating the message
11. An acronym or neumonic
12. A question to elicit their understanding
13. A step-by-step guide
14. Humour
15. A demonstration
16. A YouTube video
17. A testimonial from a salesperson
18. A photograph
19. Acting out a scene
20. Showing them the real thing

On our visit to France next year, I've been shown an app for my phone that will literally translate in French anything I speak into it in English. How cool is that? But it kinda destroys the whole fun of trying my hardest, making myself appear foolish and building a strong rapport because I'm trying my hardest to communicate. And in France there are only three words you need – du vin, du pain, du fromage.

The art of making some simple to understand

Isn't that exactly what we want to do when talking with salespersons or when presenting to a group?

Here's how:

- Clearly describe what they need to hear only; not what you think they need to know about your topic. There's a big difference.

- Then gives lots of examples. They accelerate understanding, relate to people's worlds, and make the unfamiliar...familiar.

- Finally, make sure you provide lots of visual, even if it is a flipchart drawing.

Why is it sometimes, you just get things, you understand something? These three steps will let you have the same power.

Let 'em get on with it

I was watching reruns recently of the music programme from the 1970s – *The Old Grey Whistle Test* – and I listened intently to Bob Harris, one of the show's originators, telling us the secret to its success.

"We brought the band into a tiny studio, gave them lighting, all the equipment they needed, and a camera...and asked them to perform anything they wanted for ten minutes."

And this strategy produced some of the country's prolific live music sequences; they're still playing them today on BBC4.

For us sales managers and coaches, maybe we should let go more often. Give them the tools, the space to perform, and the stage, and let 'em get on with it.

I think we'll be amazed as to what people will produce if we let them shine.

The Perils of "Should"

I have three wonderful children, not always so wonderful I can tell you. Who has children here? As a parent, my job is to provide guidance and a paternalistic attitude to help them grow up and become great adults. Well, that's the job anyway.

And over the years I've done just that, sharing my experience, wisdom, knowledge, and mistakes to my growing children. But this holiday in August, it all kinda went wrong, and I couldn't nail what I was doing wrong, as I hadn't changed at all.

So what was going wrong on holiday?

Two weeks in a static caravan on the beautiful French coast of the Vendee. Miles and miles of white sandy beaches, gorgeous weather, and great food, couldn't get better. Unless of course you had my three children. Now aged fifteen, thirteen, and nine, they regarded a holiday as exactly that…a holiday, a break from the norm when they could relax and take life easy.

On a self-catering holiday you all have to pull your weight and they weren't, so I gave them my experience, wisdom, and knowledge. Did it work? No way. We ended arguing and fighting. So I played the nice card, the bribery card since I held the stash of Euros. That one worked for a few days, but my money ran out. I played the "Come on, guys, do it for your mother" card, and that didn't work. I was at a loss. This hadn't happened to me before as a father. I thought I was a decent dad, bringing them up, providing, looking after them, but here on holiday in France it was all going Pete Tong.

Meanwhile Claire, my wife, had noticed, and that evening she confided in me. My wife knows me. Well, you would after being with someone for almost twenty years. She knows my ways and doesn't often interfere, but I could see in her eyes she wanted to say something. "Go on," I said, inviting the feedback, "what are you seeing?"

Clare explained that what I was doing was not working. The children were growing up. After all, Lewis was fifteen and almost a grown-up, although some would disagree. "Okay", she continued, "your style worked when they were younger, growing up, seeking guidance, feeling their way in the world. But not now, when they want to discover themselves and make mistakes and learn in a non-directive manner." Claire explained that she'd been noticing for a while, but I was just too busy, always rushing around, busy at work…for her to tell me. But here in relaxing France was as good a time as any.

The following day I noticed exactly what Claire had been saying, I heard myself saying it without noticing its impact, so I started not using it. Crikey, it was difficult at first. I had to stop and change my words, my language, my meaning. The children's faces were remarkable, as though I was from another planet; you know the "urggh" look. The next few days, things cooled. The children started pulling their weight helping, being fun, and the holiday lived happily ever after.

Where was I going wrong? I kept using one word too much in my vocabulary. Should. I was always, "You should do this, you should do that. You shouldn't do it that way, you should do it like this."

Just one six-letter word was making all the impact. Okay, when they were young it was fine. They needed guidance and they took it from Dad. It helped them, framed them. But as they grew older into adulthood, it just wound them up, infuriated hem, constrained them.

Now of course, should is not just a word but a style of communication, a way of influencing people, helping people, guiding people. It has excellent intentions but falls flat on an audience who doesn't want to be told what to do. And that was my three children.

My intention, I think, was worthy; even Claire admitted this. But the outcome, the meaning was not right.

So what about you? Have you ever been caught using this word or its meaning too much, with all the very best intentions? Have you used "should"?

Can we learn from Uttar Pradesh?

Improving healthcare is a costly business, right? It doesn't have to be, says Jeremy Laurance. In fact, we could save a lot of lives and money with just a single sheet of A4 paper. A checklist. That is the lesson from Uttar Pradesh in India, where rates of maternal and newborn deaths have been slashed simply as a result of issuing maternity staff with a checklist of 29 vital tasks to be performed at every birth – handwashing, taking the mother's blood pressure, and so on.

Compulsory use of checklists was a practice initiated in the aviation industry: it helped ensure pilots made the essential cockpit tests.

Could we use more checklists? Here' some ideas

- In sales coaching, have a checklist of skills to be looking out for.

- Have a checklist with GROW and suggested questions to open up the coachee.

- Checklist your sales process so your salespeople can ensure they cover everything they need to.

I'm sure you have more ideas.

Such a simple concept.

Achievement Coaching

How to be an Achievement Coach

The whole point of coaching is to generate some action from the client towards whatever their goal is. Coaching is not to fix people; if you think your client needs fixing then you are wrong. Never assume someone is damaged. They may have limiting beliefs or other blocks to their success and you can handle these when they arrive in the coaching sessions.

The other mistake coaches make is to launch too soon into goal setting and the ubiquitous GROW model. GROW is awe-inspiring, I use it all the time once a goal has been emotionally charged, set properly and chunked down to the one main goal that will achieve everything, the one thing that the client needs to focus on.

Allow me to outline my template for an Achievement Coaching Session with clients, including the high impact first session.

1. Induction – set frames, what is coaching, expectations, definition of achievement coaching and guarantees.

2. Purpose in life exercise to determine the client's real purpose and to align this later with their goals. Its' useful to test whether the goal and actions they depend on later are "on purpose" – it gives direction and bags of energy.

3. Identify blockages that may exist which prevent achieving the goal and outcome wanted by the client. Spinning plates exercise to reveal the paraphernalia that may be preventing clarity of thinking. Do a belief change exercise if the client has some limiting beliefs that need to be dealt with.

4. Values of the client, either through the online SDI – Strength Deployment Inventory (my preference), or the general "What's important to you about…" questions. These create emotional engagement and allow for the motivation behind the goal – a crucial element.

5. Strengths of the client exercise to determine what they are good at, which links nicely to the SDI. What they do best exercise around these strengths.

6. Goal setting and action plan. The client gets to settle on their goal, we set it properly using SMART, but we use:

    ▪ Specific

    ▪ Meaningful (to you)

    ▪ Act as if

    ▪ Realistic

    ▪ Towards (not away from)

    We then place the goal with the client into their future timeline. If the goal is a "someday" goal, we reduce it to the one thing that they can achieve that has a domino effect on the rest of the goals. We then help the client to focus on the one thing eliminating any reticence to have a Plan B – which is the greatest hindrance to achieving goals.

That's the template; it works, although it may be different to the usual "What's your goal?" and "Let's GROW it and chase you up to see if you've done your agreed actions". Achievement coaching gets alarmingly good results, but remember, guarantees are only given if the client does as they say they will in their actions.

The Responsibility Lies with the Coachee

When my son Euan was younger, he played for a junior rugby team and I helped to coach them alongside other keen and enthusiastic dads.

We were a reasonable team, but not brilliant. I think the quality of the coaches was also in question, but we sought ways to improve. Serendipity provided the answer. Let me explain.

At the club's annual dinner, we were donated a rugby ball from Gloucester Rugby's 2005 winning team. An actual match ball used by top players. You know; it had been felt, passed and caught by real players. The ball went into the auction as the top prize.

Let me fast-forward the story, because you've guessed it, we won the ball.

I thought that's it, at last we can play like winners, so I introduced the ball at our next training session and used it for the match against Kidderminster.

Did the ball make a difference? Not a bit. We lost handsomely.

A ball is not going to make any difference. Responsibility for performance lies with the players and the coaching team; we hadn't improved and a new ball wasn't going to make any difference.

In the same way, responsibility in coaching lies with the coachee, not the coach.

Life Purpose Exercise

Internal Drive Inventory

Go through the entire list of words on the next page and circle all the items that give you a strong positive kinaesthetic. Pick the top three or four themes that have the greatest kinaesthetic or meaning to you. Remember, there are no correct answers, and the meaning of each word or phrase is for you to determine.

- Personal achievement
- Happiness
- Earning money
- Loving someone (others)
- Being loved, being accepted
- Popularity
- Competence
- Independence
- Risking
- Being different
- Being your best
- Reaching your potential
- Finding excitement
- Being a leader
- Learning, gaining wisdom
- Gaining mastery
- Making a worthwhile contribution
- Fully expressing yourself
- Becoming an expert
- Making a positive difference
- Winning
- Finding the good in others
- Gaining recognition
- Building something
- Gaining the approval of others
- Creating something
- Getting things done
- Doing good
- Dominating
- Being unique
- Being the best
- Gaining security, safety
- Controlling
- Having fun
- Working hard
- Having influence over others
- Experiencing life to its fullest
- Seeking adventure
- Power, authority
- Prestige

Internal Drive History

List at least one accomplishment in each age category listed below that gave you the greatest sense of joy. These are accomplishments that you personally felt good about regardless of what others thought at the time.

In addition to listing these accomplishments, answer the questions to further identify the important aspects of each. (If you don't get an answer right away, don't dwell on it. It probably doesn't apply to your situation.)

Age 18 - 22

- What was the activity?
- What did you actually do?
- What specifically was the sense of joy?
- What abilities were demonstrated by the accomplishment?
- What was the general subject matter?
- What were the circumstances?
- What were the relationships to other people and things?

Age 23 - 30

- What was the activity?
- What did you actually do?
- What specifically was the sense of joy?
- What abilities were demonstrated by the accomplishment?
- What was the general subject matter?
- What were the circumstances?
- What were the relationships to other people and things?

Age 31 - 40

- What was the activity?
- What did you actually do?
- What specifically was the sense of joy?
- What abilities were demonstrated by the accomplishment?
- What was the general subject matter?
- What were the circumstances?
- What were the relationships to other people and things?

Age 41 - 50

- What was the activity?
- What did you actually do?
- What specifically was the sense of joy?

- What abilities were demonstrated by the accomplishment?

- What was the general subject matter?

- What were the circumstances?

- What were the relationships to other people and things?

Internal drive summary

Once you've completed the history questions, please answer the following summary questions:

1. Throughout your life, what activity has consistently produced the greatest sense of joy?
2. What skills or abilities do you most like to perform?
3. What do you most like about yourself?
4. What patterns, trends, or consistencies do you observe in your answers so far?

Describing yourself when on purpose

The goal is to create a description of what you are like when you are demonstrating your purpose. Complete the following in as much detail as possible.

1. What are you doing when you experience the greatest sense of self-fulfilment?
2. Who are you being when you experience the greatest sense of joy?
3. Describe the visual images you see when you are being this person.
4. Describe what it feels like to be this person.
5. Describe the things you say to yourself when you are being this person.

Devote some time to these important questions and review your answers periodically to make additions or deletions as you discover new and important things about yourself and your sense of purpose.

Your Statement of Purpose

The goal is to create a set of words that causes you to deeply feel what your life is about.

Take the information from the above exercises and use the combination of words and phrases to draw up a statement of purpose that has the strongest meaning and deepest emotional feeling for you.

Don't worry about the statement being grammatically correct for now. Your statement of purpose could have as little as one word or as many as is necessary to create a strong emotional feeling deep within.

The key is to come up with a definite theme that best describes the driving force in your life that you can review regularly and that provides you with a strong emotional charge each time you read it.

What do you do best?

1. What part of your work do you most enjoy?
2. What aspect of your work gives you the greatest sense of accomplishment?
3. What aspect of your work are you best at?
4. What were you doing when you were having the most fun at work?
5. What type of people are you most comfortable with?
6. How would you describe the values of these people?
7. What part of your business brings you the greatest sense of joy and accomplishment?
8. What prospecting approach has consistently been the most successful for you in the past?

Energy Sappers

You want success. Everything that is ongoing will drain energy from you. You may not know it but the leak is going on 24 hours a day. Just like plate spinning, you have to run around to keep pumping energy into the plates to prevent them falling off.

Energy Sapper	Yes/No	When by?
1. Make a list of the things you have to do – a To Do list – refer to it daily.		
2. Get an Appointment Calendar – digital or paper. Put all your appointments on it – refer to it daily. Plan your time. Stick to it.		
3. Clean up your house, and or your office.		
4. Clean up your car – inside and out. Get it valeted and serviced.		
5. Throw away everything you don't use, haven't used for 6 months, or which is outdated. (Keep and file all business receipts)		
6. Organise all your papers.		
7. File or throw away any unused papers.		
8. Clean out all filing cabinets. Throw away unused materials.		
9. Clean off the top of your desk. Throw away unused materials and any unneeded papers. File all papers you don't throw away.		
10. File any past tax or business filings.		
11. Get your bank account balanced. If self-employed get all financial statements (Profit & Loss, and Balance Sheet) up to date. Keep them up to date.		
12. Pay all your bills or make arrangements and/or agreements as to when you will pay them. Keep those agreements.		
13. Make a list of everyone who owes you money, or who has borrowed things. Write or call and ask for the money (or the thing borrowed), or cross the person off the list and decide it is complete.		

14. Make a list of all the things you have started but not completed. Complete the list, or cross it off and decide not to do it.		
15. Make a list of all the things you have started, are ongoing, and which are incomplete. Complete the list, or cross it off and decide not to do it.		
16. Make a list of all the things, which have been going on for a long time, but you have just not completed. Complete the list, or cross it off and decide not to do it.		
17. Make a list of all the agreements you've made. Fulfil all past agreements. Renegotiate and make new agreements with any that you can't fulfil.		
18. Take total responsibility for your business. Do only what you can, delegate the rest. Agree only to what you know you can fulfil. Never commit to more than you know you can do.		
19. Start taking care of your physical body – eat well, exercise well, sleep well, etc.		

Belief Systems for Clients

Do you have an abundance mindset, a belief in feast? This is where you believe wholeheartedly in what you do and the immense value it brings to your clients. You offer a superior service; you do a great job and you truly are an expert in your field. This self-confidence comes with time, don't wait to receive validation from external sources or feedback…you **are** valid.

The acid test is this. If you were in the market for the service that you provide, you would buy from you, wouldn't you?

My research and work in sales fires up the following beliefs that support an abundance mindset:

1. I'm responsible for the outcomes of my role
2. I'm good at solving client problems and issues
3. I feel good about myself and my abilities
4. I have rugged self esteem
5. I'm an expert in my niche
6. I'm clear on the value that I bring to the table
7. I want to build my clients' businesses and be regarded as a trusted partner
8. I'm here to build long-term relationships with clients
9. I know I can add value to clients
10. I know what I want
11. Even if I don't make any sales, I'll feel good about my performance
12. Change is good
13. I compare very favourably with others in my field
14. I am confident in what I do
15. I believe in the bigger picture rather than the detail
16. Stepping outside my comfort zone is scary but vital for my self-development
17. I am capable of keeping abreast of all industry problems and challenges
18. I believe in sometimes asking really tough questions and enjoying the silence
19. Everything I do adds value to clients
20. I wholeheartedly believe that to grow my business I can achieve this exclusively with a proactive referral management system

The last belief is the cornerstone to being successful with referrals. If you feel you want and need to adopt this belief and own it, then here's a little bit of Neuro Linguistic Programming (NLP) to help. It's about questioning away the belief first.

Write down below your current belief around adopting and succeeding in a proactive referral system. Go on and be honest.

Now ask yourself these questions or better still, get a colleague to do so. Verbalise the answers, don't dwell on them too long; answer all the questions within 5 or so minutes. Be honest with the answers.

1. What is your limiting belief?
2. Does this belief help you?
3. What examples can you think of when your limiting belief was not true or didn't apply?
4. How is this belief ridiculous or absurd?
5. What caused you to have this belief in the first place?
6. What's the consequence of having this belief?
7. If you keep this belief, what will it cost you in the future?
8. For whom is this belief not true?
9. Do top performing professional advisers have this belief?
10. How would you know if this belief were false?
11. What was the original purpose for having this belief?
12. What do you want to believe in instead?
13. What would be the advantage to you of having this new belief?

Emotionally Charge Your Goals

People have poor memories; I know because I do. Unless I'm emotionally linked to something, I forget. This concept transcends to goal setting and the rule is simple.

We should emotionally engage our clients around their goals otherwise they won't achieve them. Relying on logic is dangerous. People don't make decisions rationally and when it comes to goals, they don't do what they say.

And that's dangerous; the whole point of coaching is that the client takes action to achieve their goals.

Decision making is driven by someone's values and emotionally charged values are electrifying when it comes to goals.

I read that Tottenham star Deli Ali was sent the latest Xbox and took a photo of himself and posted it to Instagram with the #ad. It was a classic product placement and it worked well, far superior than old fashioned advertising. We've known this for years. The latest Bond blockbuster Spectre showed a clip of Bond opening the mini bar in his room and selecting a Heineken beer. Sales shot up that month and the product promotion compared very favourably to a traditional advert.

Placement appeals to people's emotions and values. Deli Ali is a first-class footballer and plays for England and Daniel Craig is loved by millions of girls and secretly admired by men as well, who now mostly drink Heineken.

When you're coaching someone, leave the goal setting piece to the end; it should be one of the last things you do. Instead elicit the values and the emotions behind the person before you start.

The pattern is:

1. Elicit the values
2. Prioritise them
3. Find the emotions behind
4. Test

For the values of the person, find out "What's important about…"

Do a first and second wave because the first wave normally provides vast generalisation, the second wave gives better data.

Prioritise by asking: "Which one is most important?"; "And then?"

To find the emotions, ask: "Why's that?"

I did this exercise and my top 4 values for the topic of expanding my business were:

1. Enjoyment and satisfaction
2. Achievement and success
3. Trust
4. Results

By the way, a value is a noun that you cannot put into a wheelbarrow.

And when you're coaching and your client turns around and gives you some actions that you patently know are not congruent with her, challenge them by saying "Which of those options are closely aligned to your purpose and values?"

You'll then have a client that is emotionally charged towards achieving their goals.

The Perils of Plan B

My journey to Bangladesh began on the Sunday morning very early. It's a series of voyages – taxi, train, tube, airport, taxi, hotel. It can take upwards of 24 hours, door to door.

On my way to the train station, a friend asked what would I do if I missed the train? I quickly explained that I always have a plan B – a back door, an escape plan. A taxi I explained, would cost me a fortune, but it would get me to the airport.

You see a plan B, a back door, an escape plan is perfectly acceptable in business and recommended.

But not when you set your goals.

If you do, you'll not achieve them, you'll settle for your plan B or failure because you had a plan in case you failed.

Here's the secret, but don't tell anyone else because there's some contentious substance here.

Set your dream, determine what you want, then what you really need to achieve and finally decide what you're going to settle for.

When you have this goal, set it. Write it down, tell people if you wish, put it in your timeline, shove it in your unconscious brain and then take action.

You'll know what action to take if it's really set well, and I'll tell you how to set your goals properly in another article. The mistake is to consciously rack your brain to define how to achieve the goal, critiquing yourself when a plan doesn't materialise. Striving to create a "to do" list to formulate a plan. This is a mistake.

Instead let the goal percolate, improve with time, embed. Actions will sprout. You'll know.

And my journey to Dhaka that October weekend? Splendid; it all went so well, no delays and very comfortable until I arrived in Dhaka International immigration. Thank goodness for Smartphones and documents in the cloud to prove I was invited to the country. But it still took 2 hours to get through immigration. And on my birthday too!

Coach's Toolbox – Questioning

It's quicker to ask

Our new kitchen is fab, has everything you might need but the new dishwasher is so quiet you can't hear when it's on and that's a problem. It's a problem because I've opened it a few times right in the middle of a cycle and got soaked as punishment.

So I ask Claire, because she knows and it's quicker to ask. But that's another problem, first she's getting annoyed with me constantly asking and second, I'm not discovering the answer myself.

And in the workplace, this causes countless problems for sales coaches. You see, people ask us questions because it's quicker and easier to ask and convenient for you to just give the answer. That's not coaching and doesn't help people to develop. The answer is to take a leaf out of Claire's book. Let me explain.

Claire taught me how to spot whether the dishwasher is on. I learnt that when the dishwasher is on, there's a red light projected to the floor. Have a look.

Do I feel empowered? Not really, but it saves me asking next time.

So next time someone keeps asking you questions, before you instinctively answer, stop yourself and say:

"I'd like to help you but am pre-occupied with ...but if you tell me what you plan I'll give you some immediate feedback"

Really works that one just like our new dishwasher and that dinky little red light. How clever.

The Fallacy of Open Questions

Open questions versus closed questions—this battle has been fought for years and no one is the clear winner. However, a good open question does lend itself to a fuller answer from your salesperson. But the trick is to know how to follow up.

Anyway here's a reminder of the six open questions from Rudyard Kipling's famous poems:

"I keep six honest serving men

(They taught me all I knew);

Their names are What and Why and When

And How and Where and Who"

The dangerous one here is "why", proven to be antagonistic and annoying to the receiver. When faced with the "why" question, many salespersons will raise their defences as they feel as though they are being attacked.

Interesting.

The other problem with questions is shown by the rest of Kipling's poem:

"I know a person small -

She keeps ten million serving men,

Who get no rest at all!

She sends 'em abroad on her own affairs,

From the second she opens her eyes -

One million Hows, Two million Wheres,

And seven Million Whys!"

Care we don't turn into a military interrogator.

Coaching questioning and probing

Function	Probe	Definition	Characteristics	Use to
Getting coachee to open up	Open-end probes	Questions or requests that get wide-ranging response on a broad subject	Usually begin with – what, how, tell me. Involve coachee by letting him tell what he knows or thinks.	Open up silent coachee.
	Focused questions	Designed to probe deeper on an issue	Focus on a subject. "That's interesting what you said about…"	Get more information on a specific subject.
Getting the coachee to keep on talking	Pauses	Short silences that let coachee mull over and respond to what he's heard	Relax pace so coachee doesn't feel pressured. Let you collect thoughts and plan. Excellent for tight-lipped coachees.	Encourage silent coachees to respond.
	Verbal and non-verbal nods	Short statements that encourage coachee to keep talking	Maintain good rapport. Usually produce additional information.	Encourage coachee to amplify brief responses.
	Closed-end questions	Questions worded to produce short, precise answers	Excellent for getting final commitment and gathering details.	Focus on specifics and control roaming. Helps you learn details and fill in gaps.
Making sure you understand	Summary statements	Statements that summarise information obtained from coachee	Focus on facts, not emotions. Help coachee clarify own thinking by hearing it summed up by you.	Summarise, then deal with them one by one. Gratify coachee's esteem by showing you're listening. Focus on relevant facts. Separate wheat from chaff.

Questions types to avoid

Leading

When a coach asks a question that implies an answer, he can lead the coachee towards a solution rather than help the coachee find his own solution. The hidden answer is what the coachee *hears*.

"Have you considered…?" (i.e., "You should…")

"How could you get your manager to listen more?" (i.e., "Your manager needs to listen more.")

Multiple

This is when the coach asks more than one question at a time.

Regardless of whether they are powerful questions or not, multiple questions cause confusion. The coachee does not know which one to answer and often only answers the last one!

Why?

Questions that start with "Why…?" are best avoided… Why?!

Long-winded

They just confuse. Keep it short and simple—KISS.

Then just sit back and keep quiet; learn to love the silence.

Beware the Machine Gun Question

You might remember the Iraq War Enquiry earlier this year here in the UK. Someone who did come out smelling of roses was our very own Tony Blair.

He presented himself well, gave an assured performance, wriggled a bit when asked to recall what he said to TV presenter Fern Britton but answered the questions well. He was well-planned as you would expect from a man of his calibre.

One of the reasons he did well was the general poor quality of questions used by the panel. The question type that caused them the most problems was the machine gun question.

Time after time, they hit Tony with machine gun questions which rattled off two or three questions with one pull of the trigger, and what did Tony do? Took his time and answered the last question in the string, which was usually the easiest question to answer.

And that's what people do. They can't remember the first one or second or even the third question. They only recall and answer the last one. And those lovely questions earlier are wasted.

On analysis, the first question in the machine gun string was the better-quality question but was lost in the mist.

The panel wasted so many questions that might have made Tony wriggle some more, but they chose machine gun ones instead.

In selling, we ask questions; in coaching we ask questions, so we're missing a trick if we get caught by this one. So if you find yourself stringing questions along in a machine gun way, stop, pick a really good question, and ask it. Stop and wait for the reply.

If only the panel facing Tony Blair had done that, who knows what the outcome would have been.

Coaches leading the witness

Watching the Michael Jackson trial on TV recently reminds me of a common error from newly trained sales coaches. And at first glance it appears the new coaches are doing the right thing.

Let me explain.

Many sales manager positions are filled by the top-performing salespeople. It seems a simple choice really. Promote your best salespeople into a sales manager and sales coach position. After all, they can guide the new breed in the right way to do the job since they can do it.

We all know the problems this can cause as management is vastly different from selling.

The alarm bells begin to ring when the newly promoted managers start coaching. New sales coaches are trained how to coach, you know, how not to tell but to ask questions instead, to draw it out of the salesperson. Self-discovery questions—the need to haul out the answer from them.

So they're stuck between a rock and a hard place.

On one hand, they're keen just to tell the salesperson how to do their job better because they know the answer. On the other hand they know they have to ask questions to let the salesperson come out with the answer.

So they start asking "leading the witness" questions. Bring back Michael Jackson's lawyers in the courtroom.

"You were at the scene of the crime, weren't you?"

"How did you use poison to kill the victim?"

"I put it to you that you poisoned the victim."

Designed to make the witness head in a certain direction, and this is what I hear coaches use as well.

"When you closed the sale, what could you have done better?"

"What about your opening sound bite? What was not working there?"

Salespeople aren't stupid. The salesperson will just close down. They'll refuse to play ball and will just wait for the coach to tell them. And the coach tells them.

Not good coaching.

Instead use real exploratory questions to examine the salesperson's performance post the observation.

"What parts of the meeting went the best for you?"

"Let's break it up into three parts – open, explore, close. Let's start with the opening. How did your salesperson react to your opening?"

I must say, I do admire those lawyers in the courts; it all looks very theatrical to me. Maybe that's why they televise them in the States. Perhaps it's just theatre!

Potholing and Power Questioning

"You need a hobby" were the last words from my wife's mouth as I left on an overseas trip. You see, I'd been working all weekend preparing for my talk, which is wrong, foolish, and not good for the soul. Fortunately, on the plane, I browsed one of those flight magazines and came across an article on potholing. Fascinating

Now if you coach people or ask questions as part of your job, then you need to think about potholing.

Let me explain.

If you ask questions as a coach or consultative salesperson, you need to ask good questions, not dumb ones. Obvious that, really. Dumb questions get you nowhere. They're often leading or multiple questions or just plain dumb.

In potholing this is where you aim down a narrow dead-end. You have no choice but to retrace your steps back to where you started.

In potholing, if you find the right route, you can be rewarded with a cavern of stalagmites and stalactites, wondrous scenery and numerous **further vistas** to explore. Faced with this cavern, you just have to keep exploring.

The same in coaching. Power questions give you enormous amounts of information and colour that allow you to continue exploring. **A powerful question is expansive and opens up further routes to explore for the coach.** A power question is one where you get that look from your coachee or client. They're saying to themselves, "That's a good question." They look up and ponder the answer. And because you're good at listening and nodding, they give you an enlightened answer, which by the mere process of verbalising it, has given them colossal value.

Here's some tips to help you ask Power Questions:

- Make them short. Cut out all unnecessary words and don't string them together.

- Ask curious questions that evoke personal exploration, not just information.

- Go very quiet when you've asked them; revel in the silent seconds.

Here are some especially powerful questions:

- What is your desired outcome?

- What do you want?

- Where do we go from here?

- How will you know?

- What will that get you?

- What do you need to say no to?

When I returned home a few days later armed with gifts for the whole family, I announced the best present of all. "I'm going to join a potholing club – the Gloucester Speleological Society. I've Googled them and they are welcoming new members."

And the response? Well, I daren't tell you. It's not publishable. Oh well, back to the drawing board for my hobby.

How to Sugarcoat your questions

Beware the Rising Tone

"It's called early teenage talk."

That was the response from a teenage expert after I asked about the irritating habit I've noticed my teenage son using when talking to his friends. "It's called teenage talk."

So what is this annoying habit that causes me to moan about?

It's the constant rising tonality of every sentence that my son uses. His sentences start normal and then his voice rises at the end of the phrase or sentence. This continues for hours. Have you noticed it from people?

Now it's not going to harm anyone, and I should move on to worry about more important things, but it actually is important in sales. More than people think.

We all know that communication is more than just the words chosen. Plenty of research carried out over the last thirty years shows that face-to-face communication consists of three parts – the words, the way you say them and the body language that's used to launch the words. The tone of the voice has a remarkable influence on the meaning, more than we think.

Straightforward really. A flat tone tells you that the sentence is just a statement. A falling tone indicates a command and a rising sentence says there is a question here.

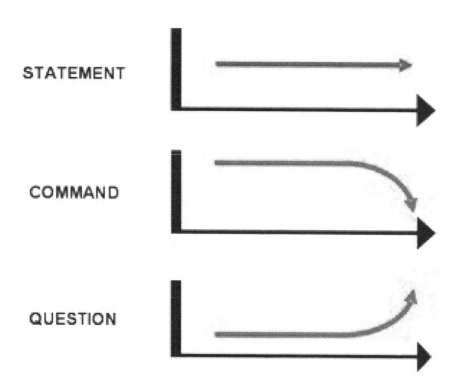

Try it now. Say something like, "It's time to go to bed." Say it with a flat, falling, and then a rising tone and listen to the impact. It really works, doesn't it?

Secondly, when you want your salesperson to do something, drop your tone a little but only just a little.

Pre-framing

Gosh, that's a terrible title, don't you think? Pre-framing…sounds like something you do in the shower!

But it can be really useful when selling on the telephone, especially when asking questions. The theory works like this. Humans like to be told what's coming up next, in other words to be pre-conditioned, so when it happens it's not so much of a shock.

Let me give you an example. Many moons ago when I worked in estate agency, we had a property that refused to sell. Admittedly it was a little rundown, in need of some urgent tender loving care, but a decent house for the price. But it refused to shift, and we couldn't realize why, until we had some feedback from a buyer who said that the roads on the way in were awful and just put them off before they even got to the house. So when they arrived at the home, they were pre-conditioned to not like it.

So the next applicant who was interested to have a look was swiftly put in the manager's BMW and driven to the house. Admittedly it was the long way there, but the journey we chose was much more amenable and pleasant and put the applicant in the best frame of mind to view the house.

And it worked too!

Another practical tip is to use pre-conditions in your language when presenting to salespersons. I like to use the phrase, "I've left the best for last"…and "here it is" or "and here's the best news…"

You see, you're pre-conditioning the next part of your statement, and this is a really useful technique when asking questions that are a little tough.

"Mr. Brown, would you be able to tell me please…."

"I hope you're okay for me to ask…"

"May I ask…."

"I'd be curious to know…."

"I'd be very interested to know…"

"Tell me…"

Here's how to avoid a trap I often hear salespeople fall into. Don't pre-condition negatively, for example:

"I'm sorry to ask this…."

"We have to talk about the cost now I'm afraid."

"I hope you don't mind me asking but…"

You see, you're simply negatively pre-conditioning them with your language.

A state of curiosity

My father visited us this Christmas; I hadn't seen him for over a year and was very keen to catch up, particularly as his life has been extremely tumultuous over the last twelve months. Relationships, moving to France, journeys, people…his life is very complex, and I was dying to find out everything. You simply can't extract these things on Facebook or even on Skype, so I thought a wholesome meal and a glass or two of a good red wine would loosen his tongue.

Boy, was I in a state of curiosity.

And it worked a treat; my questions were subtle, delving, curious without being interrogational. I was in top form on the listening stakes, not judging him or butting in with too many questions. Yes, the wine helped, but it was my intense state of curiosity that helped the most.

I'm going to recall this moment as vividly as I can. Next time I need to operate as an effective coach because it changes my state from normal to a state of curiosity, and that will help me craft better questions and listen more powerfully.

So think of a time in your past when you were amazingly curious to find out something, sink the story into your main memory, and recall it whenever you need to change your state. I will use that illuminating Christmas evening this year.

And I thought my life was exciting, you ought to hear the details of my father's who's going to turn seventy-four this summer.

Do you have a solution filter?

Are you constantly solutioneering?

The modern business world is full of metrics, KPIs, results, percentages, and we're berated if we don't have solutions to problems quickly, practical ones that we can evoke immediately to give business a profit boost.

"I don't want problems. I want solutions," yells the managing director

Sound familiar?

It's this context in which many coaches find themselves, particularly frontline coaches with hectic timetables and results-oriented targets. And when faced with this scenario, as we coach with the intention of listening and helping the coachee find solutions, we listen with a solution filter.

We don't mean to, but as we listen, we figure out a solution. It's built into our DNA to do this and makes us impatient to listen, wanting to move on to solution stage as soon as we can.

This is dangerous, especially when the coachee would benefit hugely from discovering the solution themselves.

Instead switch off your solution filter, listen in the moment, don't think about what the coachee is saying, just hear them. Listen to their point of view, their issues, problems…hear what they are saying, how they are saying it. Try to read between the lines with the emotions and non-verbal signals. Use your intuition. Don't interrupt them. Don't follow up with another question too early. Just hear them, appreciate them, and play back what they just said before moving onto the next stage.

So next time you're in a coaching situation, is your solution filter at the ready? It often is with me, and I have to switch it off deliberately and move into the moment with my listening.

It works – try it.

Plan your rescue question

Here's a tale that many parents will relate to and gives some thought to help at the next sales meeting.

It was rush hour and I was travelling on a packed intercity train, and in the opposite seat was a young couple with a toddler who was causing all sorts of commotion. The poor young couple were very embarrassed. The carriage was stony quiet except for the toddler, and everyone was staring at the young couple.

Along came the conductor to check tickets, and to the rescue she came. She soon realised how uncomfortable the couple were so offered to head back to the buffet car where they had some special toddler packs containing colouring pencils and picture books. The couple were even more self-conscious being asked a question until the elderly chap next to me said, "Oh, can I have one as well please?"

He laughed, followed by everyone else, and the icy tension quickly thawed.

He had rescued the situation with some quick thinking and humour.

This made me think about sales meetings and the need to have one or two questions up your sleeve as rescue questions. When the situation gets tricky – maybe your salesperson has said something that completely throws you or your laptop crashes right in the middle of the presentation – most of us can't think quickly enough to come out with an appropriate response, so have one prepared. It's here that you can use your rescue question to get you out of the tricky mess.

Here are a few ideas:

"That's a good point – can we park that and come back later?"

"Tell me about your year so far."

"What major changes are you implementing this year?"

So memorise some rescue questions just in case – you never know when they'll come in handy.

And the toddler? Sure enough, the toddler pack did the trick but only for ten minutes. I felt very sorry for the couple but reached for a twenty-first-century gadget to get me out of bother – my iPod, and drowned out the noise.

Coach's Toolbox – Body Language

The problem with studying body language

One big problem with the study of body language is the speed with which people can make an assumption based on one signal. The common example is when people cross their arms. Aficionados of body language would say that they are being defensive and possibly angry inside.

Rubbish. They might just be cold or might want to hide their middle-age paunch. We should be looking for clusters of signals before we start to make judgments.

A neat little body language model

A neat little model will help us here to see these clusters of signals before we make a judgment.

The model consists of two dimensions. Open to closed and forward to back and looks like this:

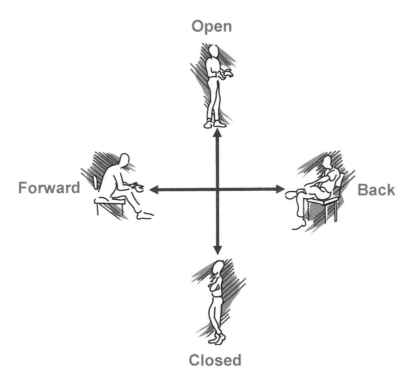

The model is clever because it allows us to cluster signals to determine what the person is thinking. For example, someone who is closed and leaning back will be showing dozens of signals.

Crossed arms, crossed legs, leaning away, looking upwards. With such a collection of signals, we can quickly make an accurate assumption that this person is bored or tired or just doesn't want to be there. If you're in sales and your salesperson is doing this to you, then beware, you are not going to close the sale!

Let's finish off the model so you can use it as an aid memoir.

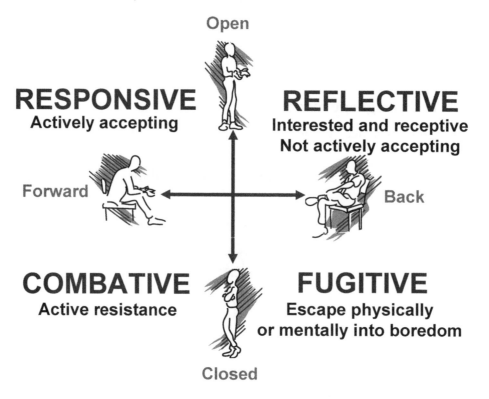

Responsive

This person is very open to what you're saying and is listening to every word. They are in full agreement with you and will be nodding and giving you plenty of eye contact.

Reflective

Here the person is interested but is probably thinking about what you are saying. They may need time to reflect or may have some questions to ask.

Fugitive

Bored, doesn't want to be there, not listening and probably daydreaming. Stop what you're doing. Ask some questions and get some feedback. Take a break. Offer them some coffee. Do something, anything to break the cycle, otherwise you're going to be unsuccessful in the coaching session.

Combative

Not good. The person may be argumentative and will want to challenge you somehow. They don't agree what you are saying and have some real issues about it.

Beware your leakage

Cold yet bright, London can be a great city to do business in. But eventually we all like to get home. Except I'd missed my train by a whisker. Now trains run from Paddington Station to Cheltenham every two hours, so I had a long wait.

So I settled down to a long, strong coffee at Starbucks and began to watch people. I love watching people, recognizing their body language, guessing what they're thinking. Don't you just love that pastime?

In walked this young chap, and he began to queue, looking at the various coffees and goodies he could buy when he caught sight of the extremely good-looking girl sitting in the corner sipping her latte.

What I saw was amazing – not the girl but the boy's body language, which reacted dramatically as a summer storm. His eyes widened, a big smile appeared, and his stomach shrank as be pulled his stomach in and his chest out. His body language showed leakage.

I call it leakage when someone suddenly changes their body language for a reason – it really is quite spectacular when it happens and can be very useful in selling and coaching.

It's useful to know about leakage for yourself and for your clients. Observing your client's leakage is vital if you want to look for non-verbal buying signals, which I always believe are the best ones. The body never lies but people have been known to tell them instead.

Use "test" closing to check for body language leakage. "How does that sound?" or "What do you think so far?" Watch them carefully for those sudden changes. Focus on the face as that's where we can't hide our feelings. Calibrate what normal looks like for them and compare with the leaked facial expressions and you can tell instantly whether they're happy or not or want to buy from you or not.

Be aware of your own leakage as well. When you're presenting to clients and you're posing a tricky question, don't give away your position by leaking your body language. Ask someone what happens to you when you are put under some pressure and learn to mask this the next time it happens. I've often seen this with people who are presenting in public and get a difficult moment, such as a question, or their remote breaks down, or they forget what to say next.

Leakage observation can also help you if you want to see how someone reacts to you. Now this chap in Starbucks would have been better off if he kept his eye on the pretty girl as her body language leaked as well. She couldn't keep her eyes off him, and her leakage was striking. If only he'd read my piece and glanced at her — they might have had a great future together. But instead he left with his skinny latte in a rather rushed manner. The innocence of youth, or is it body language naivety?

Body Language Quiz

Finally, let's have a little quiz to see how sharp you are with your body language recognition. Here are some pictures of typical clusters. Under each one is a description of the cluster and the possible interpretation. Have a look at each one and decide your interpretation before you reveal yours. See how close you get.

Good luck.

Defensiveness

Arms crossed on chest; can also be a sign of disagreement.

Closed fists; can also be a sign of nervousness.

Facial expressions a bit obvious.

Openness

Open hands with palms upward. Arms and legs not crossed.

Evaluation

Hand-to-cheek gestures

An interested person leans forward, head slightly tilted, supported by one hand.

A critical evaluation is given with the hand brought up to the face. The chin is in the palm, and index finger is extended along the cheek, and the remaining fingers are positioned below the mouth.

A tilted head is a definite sign of interest.

Stroking the chin indicates a thinking or evaluation process.

The body leaning forward is a sign of interest.

Suspicion and Secretiveness

A person who won't look at you is likely concealing something.

Touching or rubbing the nose, usually with the index finger, is a sign of doubt or non-truth on the part of the speaker.

Rubbing behind or beside the ear with the index finger when weighing an answer indicates doubt.

Honesty

Hand over heart

Frustration

Short breaths; people who are angry take short breaths and expel air through their nostrils.

Tightly clenched hands

Wringing hands

Confidence

Steepling (hands or arms brought together to form a church steeple)

Contemplation

Hands joined together behind the body.

Typical catapult position

Leaning back in a seated position with both hands supporting head.

Confidence, maybe arrogance

Nervousness

Playing with pencils, notebooks, or eyeglasses in mouth.

Boredom

Drumming table

Tapping with feet

Head in hand

Promote positive body language

Relaxed posture - comfortably seated, relaxed breathing, no visible stiffness or abrupt movements. These indicate no major barriers to communication.

- Arms relaxed - uncrossed arms and hands open (palms up or otherwise visible to the other person) are signs of openness.

- Good eye contact

- Nodding agreement - when nods are used to punctuate key things the other person has said, they signal agreement, interest, and understanding. However, continual unconscious bobbing of the head usually indicates that the listener is tuning out.

- Smiling/adding humour - this is a very positive sign. It signals a warm, personal relationship.

- Leaning closer - reducing the distance between two people, particularly when the other person is speaking. Indicates interest is up and barriers are down.

- Gesturing warmly - talking with hands, particularly with palms open, indicates involvement in the conversation and openness to the other person.

Beware negative body language

Actions that are generally considered negative may just be a matter of comfort for this person, may indicate that the person is tired, or may result from other matters that are weighing on this person's mind.

- Body tense - Stiffness, wrinkled brow, jerky body motion, hands clasped in front or palms down on the table.

- Arms folded in front - creates a barrier; can express resistance to what is being said.

- Hand on face - a hand over one's mouth is a closed gesture. Leaning on one's elbow with the chin in the hand can communicate boredom.

- Fidgeting - moving around a lot, playing with things and drumming fingers are usually a sign of boredom, nervousness, or impatience.

- Impatience - trying to interrupt what the other person is saying, opening one's mouth frequently as if to speak.

- Leaning away - avoiding moving closer, even when something is handed to the person, is strongly negative.

- Negative facial expressions - these include shaking head, eyes narrowed, scowling, and frowning.

Facial language

The future is video conferencing whether we like it or not, and HD technology means we have to start focusing on our facial body language to maximise our message. Let me show you how an old TV can help.

Our TV is only six years old, but the kids reckon it's ancient. *"Belongs in a museum, Dad."* Now I'm not going to change the set until it packs up on us. That's the way I am, but the children kept badgering me to look at the new breed of flat-screen high-definition 3D tellies.

Whilst in Currys buying some stuff for my computer, I happened across their huge range of new TVs. Euan was with me, so we thought we'd have a look. And it blew me away. Screen after screen all paraded along the wall in their fifty-inch-plus glory. A wonderful site, and I was soon fixated on one demo TV which cleverly showed a split screen. Glued I was.

One-half was old-fashioned TV, like ours at home, showing all the graininess of a crisp bread. The other half was HD at its finest. I could even see a bead of sweat on the actor's face and the blushing of his cheeks. I read somewhere that the new breed of TVs are making actors go back to drama school as they have to relearn how to use all the expressions of their faces when acting, rather than the obvious forms of body language. The camera is getting closer and picks out every minute detail, and the actors have to prepare for this.

And then I started thinking about salespeople and their managers appearing on these screens in the form of modern video conferencing, telepresence, web conferences, GoToMeeting, etc. How good are we at using your face when communicating? In coaching and close-up selling, the face can give away all sorts of clues to how we're feeling and what's on our mind.

Are you aware of every expression you use, how you flush when you get worked up, your eye movements, beads of sweat? Are you aware of your body language leakage, in other words when you show a sudden change in appearance? Close-up face-to-face communication and on a big screen in the near future, your audiences will pick this up.

Facial language tips

So here's some quick tips and reminders on facial body language and the effect:

- Eye contact - on a screen your eye contact should be steadier than normal and only look away for an effect.

- Gazing regularly shows a positive, inviting attitude – open to communication. Here's the area to gaze at:

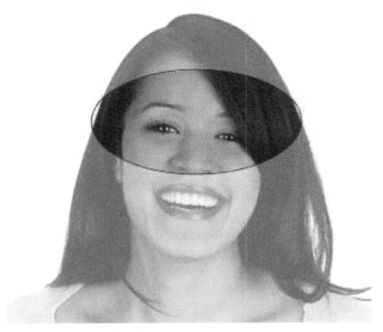

- Eye flicker shows nerves and tiredness.

- Nodding occasionally while this person is talking to you shows you are interested and focused on them.

- Tilting your head shows empathy and that you're thinking about the answer to their question.

- Shaking and nodding your head in agreement or disagreement, beware as in some countries it means the opposite.

- Tension in brow – shown by scrunching them together.

- Hand-to-face scratching indicates thought or nervousness.

- Adam's apple, mostly visible in men - a jumping Adam's apple shows anxiety, embarrassment, stress.

- Nerves shown by reddening cheeks, sweating.

- Nose flare shows agitated, angry.

- Nose twist to one side, shows disagreement or dislike.

- Pursing lips showing anger or negative thoughts.

I guess the key message is to get some training in body language. Remember that future video communications requires as much focus on our facial language as body language.

Learn to use it to your advantage. And until I upgrade my TV, we won't be seeing any detail to worry about in the Archer household.

Coaching lessons from an optician

Last week, I was invited by Tesco's optician for my bi-yearly eye appointment, and hasn't the technology and capability advanced in just two years?

With all the prodding and testing, they can now tell if you are going to get various illnesses and diseases by looking at your eyes. They can predict diabetes, glaucoma, and see if your cholesterol is heightened.

How clever, and we've always known that your eyes are the windows to your soul, which is why we need to reassess our own eye contact with our salespersons. We need to ensure we're bearing all, connecting and building trust through our eyes.

So here's a quick bi-annual eye check for you:

*   Give as much eye contact to your salesperson as they give you. Calibrate their eye contact and match it.

*   Give stronger eye contact when you're talking.

*   Less when listening, occasionally look away.

*   Gaze, don't stare.

*   Look up more as this is a general sign that you're thinking deeply on what they've just said.

*   For maximum empathy, tilt your head a tad to the left, salespersons will read this as understanding and empathy. Watch dogs, they do this with their owners to empathise.

So a quick reminder on the joy of eye contact, but no joy for me as I was diagnosed with deteriorating eyes, so I needed new glasses for reading and computer work. £200 later with two sets of glasses, I felt thankful for all those Tesco Clubcard points my wife would earn.

PS. I had an eye test appointment. If you call your salesperson meetings, appointments, then stop. Only doctors, dentists, and optometrists have them, and they produce pain.

Seating and barriers

Try to remove any barriers between you and your salesperson. Sit side-by-side, maybe in the comfy chairs in your office. At least move your chair to the corner of your desk if that's the least you can do. Physical barriers create communication barriers.

Territories and Zones

Be aware of your salesperson's requirement for territory. We are all animals deep down and don't ever lose our instincts. I once took my youngest son to a party at his friend's house. His friend's dad was a farmer and had lived on a farm all his life. I went to shake his hands, and he stood a clear five feet away and leaned his body to shake hands. Immediately after he'd finished, he leant back again.

You see, in the country people respect the space around them, whereas in the city, people are not too fussed about getting closer to you. Everyone has an intimate zone that you should never encroach unless you are their loved ones. Gauging the size of this zone is the trick. Many suitors have been slapped as a result.

People have a territory, and can carry (parts of) it around with them, especially in their cars. Zone size depends on social and environmental factors. For example, people who grew up in cities usually have smaller territories than those from the countryside. Research shows there are four zones.

The intimate zone

(Radius less than fifty centimetres) is usually reserved for close friends or relatives. Anyone else who enters this zone is likely to cause an adrenaline rush as the body prepares to defend itself. This is one reason why crowds can easily get angry.

A common way of coping with intrusion into the intimate zone (e.g. in a crowd) is to not treat the others as humans. This is the basis of the generally accepted rules for conduct on public transport.

- You are not permitted to speak to anyone, even if you know them.

- You must avoid eye contact.

- You must not show any emotion.

- If you have a book or newspaper, you must appear to be engrossed in it.

- In a lift, you must watch the floor numbers change.

The personal zone or bubble

(Radius 50 centimetres to 1¼ metres) is used when talking to friends, etc.

The social zone

(Radius 1¼ metres to 3½ metres). We stand at this distance from strangers.

The public zone

(Radius more than 3½ metres). We stand at this distance to address a group.

Touching a salesperson can sometimes help anchor encouragement or praise. However, the body has "neutral" and "hot" areas that we must be aware of. For example, the arm from elbow to shoulder is "neutral" or acceptable to touch – the arm from elbow to hand is not as it may be considered intimate and inappropriate.

Coach's Toolbox – Listening Mastery

Don't solve your salesperson's problems

This morning I made the tea and Claire was busy chatting to me about life, family, and the universe. Normally I listen patiently, usually with my mind on my own day, but don't ever tell her that.

However, I acted on instinct that morning as I had plenty of other challenges on my mind.

Let me explain.

The first topic involved Bethan, my daughter, who had a school project to complete on Austria. Claire expanded by saying that she had advised Bethan to write to the Austrian Embassy to secure information about the country. Now that's what I used to do back in 1979 when I did school projects, but we have the Internet now, so I explained to Claire that Bethan should just Google it.

Then she continued that my father had posted my mother's birth certificate because she was born in Austria during the Second World War, and that would be a great addition to the project. I immediately reacted by stating that my father shouldn't post it. Why not scan it and email the PDF?

Claire went quiet, and she said...

"Stop solving my problems and listen, will you?"

I froze, realised immediately my mistake, and wondered how many times that day coaches across the land would do the same thing. Because they have experience and knowledge, they think they can have answers to every salesperson's woes and problems. Maybe they have, but that's not the point. The point is to listen.

Just listening is often enough, being a sounding board; giving them the opportunity to vocalise their challenges is often enough for them to solve the problem themselves, and how powerful is that.

We know this, I know this, but occasionally we slip into bad habits. Naughty boy, Paul.

Tuning your listening to the next level

"Daddy, are you listening to me?" This sent me spluttering over my cornflakes and drizzling milk down my freshly ironed shirt. "I'm listening, Bethan, honest," knowing full well that I was merely looking at my daughter and hadn't followed a word she was saying.

Shame on you, Daddy.

"Sorry, Bethan, what did you say?"

"It doesn't matter now, Daddy."

Gone forever that conversation, and my daughter sulked for the rest of the breakfast, all because I simply hadn't listened. I got stuck in my own little world relating everything to me and my concerns. Although I was carrying out classic active listening gestures – you know, eye contact, face tilt, nodding, those little "uh-huhs", I wasn't really listening.

But a woman is better skilled than us men at communicating – that's been proven time and time again. And my daughter, at only five, can spot when a man isn't listening properly.

Okay, I kind of got away with it this morning over breakfast... I think... I'll wait until tonight to see if Bethan is still talking to me. But in sales you won't get away with it. You'll lose the sale, and that's not so good. Imagine if your salesperson turned round to you and said, "You're not really listening to me, are you?"

That would be a killer, wouldn't it?

When practising rapport selling, not listening properly is practically a hanging offence. So how do we really do this? Two things.

One. Kick out active listening techniques. They don't work. They're false because just by giving the impression that you're listening doesn't add up. My daughter saw straight through me this morning, and your salesperson will, too.

Two. Just know that listening is hard work and you have to concentrate on it. Someone once said to me many years ago that listening is really tough. At the time, I thought this was nonsense and argued that talking was harder. How could I have been so wrong? You have to literally concentrate on listening to get it right.

And when you do, the rewards are immense in selling. You build a rapport quickly. You find out about your salesperson – their needs, wants, desires, criteria – their problems and concerns. You know when to give benefits. You know when there's a salesperson concern coming up. You know when to close. And these things add up to selling.

So how do we do it? Think three levels of listening – a bit like a volume control on your iPod.

When you want to listen more, just turn up your volume control. I know it sounds a little bit daft, but I have this imaginary volume control in my head, and when I'm selling or consulting with clients and I want to turn up my listening, I turn up my volume control, and this tells my brain to start listening more.

My volume control has three levels – level one, two, and three.

So let me tell you about these.

Level 1 listening

Level 1 listening or internal listening is when we are listening to sounds and information around us that are just for our purposes and no one else. I recall September 11th and having to use Edinburgh airport to fly home. Great timing on my part, eh? The airport was in chaos. There were security checks everywhere, people shouting and panicking – it was a nightmare.

There I was, fully aware of what was going on and intent on getting home safely and on time. I was in level 1 listening mode, and I didn't care about anyone else. I just wanted to hear the information and sounds that would mean that I got home. I listened out for the broadcasts and particularly the word Birmingham. I kept my ears open for information that would help me and no one else.

When people talk to you, do you relate what they are saying to your experience? When someone told you they went skiing this year, did you immediately relate this to your last skiing holiday and talk about that? We've all done it, haven't we? Inadvertently, we're level 1 listening and thinking only of ourselves.

At level 1, our attention is on ourselves. We listen to the words of the other person, but the focus is on what it means to us. At level 1 the spotlight is on me – my thoughts, my judgments, my feelings, my conclusions about myself and others.

Have you ever been thinking about what you are going to say next? We all do this.

So turn up your volume control now to level 2 and feel the difference.

Level 2 listening

Level 2 listening or focused listening comes next.

At level 2 there is a sharp focus on the other person. You can see it in people's posture when they are communicating at level 2. Probably both leaning forward, looking intently at each other. There is a great deal of attention on the other person and not much awareness of the outside world.

You are beginning to see their words and reasoning on their side of the fence. You've put yourself in their shoes and in their world. The next time someone tells you about their holiday, relate their experiences to them. How they saw it, what they encountered, what feelings of excitement they had.

Your awareness is totally on the other person. You listen for their words, their expression, their emotion, everything they bring. You notice what they say, how they say it. You notice what they don't say. You see how they smile or hear the tears in their voice. You listen for what they value. You listen for their vision and what makes them energetic.

You switch off all distractions (and I know this can be difficult).

I remember one of my first sales jobs selling mortgages to clients of an estate agency in Guildford High Street. My desk was right bang in the front office by the door – not ideal. And if you want to see big windows, you only have to go as far as your nearest estate agents.

The distractions were enormous as we were on the main shopping street in town.

But you need to tune out all distractions and focus just on your client to be successful at level 2.

Now turn up your volume control to the maximum – level 3

Level 3 listening

Level 3 listening or global listening is the ultimate coach's skill.

At Level 3, you listen at 360 degrees. In fact, you listen as though you and the client were at the centre of the universe receiving information from everywhere at once. Level 3 includes everything you can observe with your senses: what you see, hear, smell, and feel – the tactile sensations as well as the atmosphere.

If Level 2 is an old dial-up modem, Level 3 is wireless broadband with no physical connections -- just a room full of digital signals. We can't see these signals, but we know they're there. Level 3 uses these invisible signals.

My wife is great at level 3 listening – in fact, research suggests that women are better at this than men.

Some wonderful research was conducted by Allan and Barbara Pease and published in their book *Why Men Don't Listen and Women Can't Read Maps*. Do buy it and enjoy over Christmas. Very light, very funny, and very revealing.

For many people this is a new realm of listening. One of the benefits of learning to listen at Level 3 is greater access to your intuition. From your intuition you receive information that is not directly observable, and you use that information just as you'd use words coming from the client's mouth. At Level 3, intuition is simply more information.

Next time, just try your level 3. Trust your intuition, your gut reaction, your sixth sense to hear what is not visibly there.

And next time I'm at the breakfast table stuck in my own little world listening to my daughter at level 1, I'll just have to turn up my imaginary volume control and listen to level 3 and see the difference in her beautiful, sparkling blue eyes.

MAP Listening Skill

Move attention away from thinking

Relax, drop down, and focus on your breathing coherently. Take away your agenda; don't think about what is being said. Just trust what you hear. Don't go into your brain, don't judge, just trust in your own ability to hear the meaning.

Be in the moment for them.

Get away from surface body language, tone, thoughts into meaning. And above all don't interrupt or do any active listing gestures of techniques.

Activate state of appreciation

Appreciate the talker, eye contact, smile, nodding…but just appreciate them and what they are saying. Don't push or force your listening on them, verbal nods, but don't say anything. React facially and with your body language. Lean back and relax and just be there for them and appreciate what they're saying.

Play back the meaning of what you heard

Now you can play back the meaning of what you heard in top-line detail. "I get a feeling", "I can sense". Offer the playback, don't judge them or impose it and they'll say if you're close. Put an imaginary stake of understanding in the middle ground.

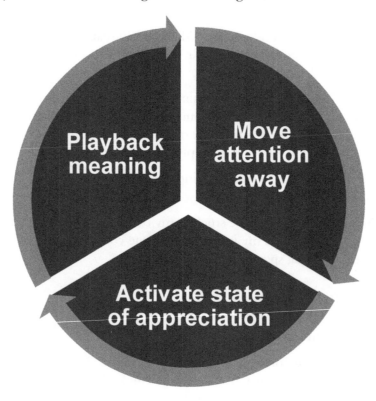

Using MAP in a GROW-based coaching session

A few years ago I arranged a one-to-one training event with a client who visited my offices for a five-hour one-to-one training session. Within ten minutes it became apparent that he was suffering with an issue, a conundrum that he needed to sort before any training could be effective.

So I decided to coach using GROW. I elicited his goal, in other words his desire to rid himself of this underlying problem, and then he just started talking...and talking...and talking.

Every sixty or so seconds, sometimes two minutes, he would pause and I'd play back what I heard, and then he started talking some more, until he paused.

I played back what I just heard and gradually steered him along the GROW sequence with a couple of questions until he arrived at some solutions, some actions to be taken which he felt would solve the problem.

It took around fifteen minutes; he spoke about ninety-five percent of the time. I asked him about three questions. The rest of my five percent was playing back what he had said.

I'd stumbled across the GROW coaching using the MAP technique, and boy, was it powerful.

Next time you're coaching and the issue is more of a problem, an issue, a conundrum, an enigma, use the following sequences of coaching:

- Goal – ask for their issue, listen, and MAP then light question to steer.

- Reality – MAP then light question to steer

- Options – MAP then light question to steer

- Will – MAP then light question to steer

Less is more, and when it comes to coach activity, this holds true.

Jim Bowen Listening

Who remembers the famous catchphrase – *super, smashing, great.*

Used by the monumental Jim Bowen from the 1980s quiz show *Bullseye*. So full of clichés and such fun. Jim was down-to-earth, serious, and ran the show like clockwork. But he kept on saying *super, smashing, great.*

After a while it became quite annoying.

What about you? Have you latched onto a phrase or string of words you're using too much? I do. These phrases can irritate people, even annoy them when overused.

Absolutely, excellent, obviously, awesome, fantastic.

They start inane and end up annoying.

So spot them, accept feedback, and stop it.

If only someone had told poor old Jim back in the day that his phrase would live on forever, for the wrong reasons, he'd never have used it. But wasn't he…super, smashing, great?

Two Diseases than inflict upon sales coaches

I am constantly amazed as to how doctors keep coming up with names for new illnesses, tags for new diseases or syndromes. And I'm also amazed when people who are given these new names feel better having a tag for their condition.

I guess it's to do with the fact that people want to be recognized as having a known predicament and a cure won't be far away.

Let me introduce you to two diseases recently recognised by sales doctors. TWT'ering and TWL'ing. And I'll also tell you two cures that can help you fight these conditions.

They are

* Thinking whilst talking – TWT

* Thinking whilst listening – TWL

The symptoms are not really listening to what's being said, ignoring what the other person is saying, being too product-centred, worrying about what question they're going to say next or what they are going to do next. The general condition is that they are just waiting to chip in, to interrupt, say something because they've heard it all before.

Advanced TWT'ering means they waffle, go through the same phrases and descriptions, sound bored, and have a very monotone voice. TWL'ers multitask whilst listening to you. You can spot one with the faint keyboard tapping in the background whilst on the phone.

Some people with the disease at advanced levels have been able to hide it very effectively by using dated active listening techniques like giving eye contact and nodding after every sentence that they've heard, and because they've been there before, heard it before, they know the answer and solution so just wait to deliver this.

In latter stages of the disease, they begin to treat their role as mundane, uneventful, and unexciting, and leave despondent.

I'm exaggerating, or am I?

The cure? Take these placebo tablets three times a day for twenty-one days and you'll be cured. The secret ingredients of the tablets are:

A drug to make you stop thinking whilst listening and talking, this drug also helps you to be in the moment with the salesperson, to hear every word they're uttering and to savour the real meaning of these. The second ingredient helps you to just be there for the salesperson, to really appreciate them, and the third prevents you from interrupting, asking another question, and makes you summarise the salesperson and ask if they've heard correctly.

Have a conversation, not an interrogation

What do newly trained coaches and my daughter have in common? Read on and I'll explain.

They keep butting in with a prepared question just after the other person is talking.

I noticed this the other day when I was assessing some newly trained sales coaches. They were so wrapped up in getting the right questions asked to achieve their GROW model or FISH model or PESOS model, or whatever they'd been taught, they forgot to listen to exactly what the other person was saying. They seemed to be butting in all the time.

My daughter does the same thing. I'm answering her question, she's not really listening, bless her, so she butts in with her next carefully thought-through question.

The message is to let your salesperson or coachee finish and then wait a second before responding. Let them finish off first. Learn to love a tiny bit of silence. Make it a conversation, not a series of questions.

I often use a traffic light in my head. When the salesperson or coachee is talking, the lights are on red. On red I say nothing but listen. When they stop talking, the light goes amber. I pause. And when the light goes green, that's when I can respond.

It's so very easy to get caught in the trap of thinking about your next question rather than listening.

A Unique Way of Pausing More

This Friday I'm finally having my two dental implants put in after treatment stretching back to 2007. It almost happened a week ago except Mike, my dentist, decided the teeth weren't quite right and sent them back for a final adjustment.

So for the last week I've been wearing a plate, otherwise known as false teeth. Now to spare you the grizzly detail and my blushes, wearing a plate is not easy. You simply can't speak for long sentences, as you have to stop, suck in, create a vacuum, and then continue. Sounds awful, I know.

But the crazy thing is this. It's helped me in my selling with clients, my consulting, and my coaching. You see, it makes me stop and pause.

Now I've always dreaded silence and would involuntarily fill it with some more words, rather than pause and let the salesperson speak or react. And I know many salespeople and coaches are the same, we just don't like silence. Any pauses sound like cavernous holes of nothing which need filling.

But due to my plate, I'm dishing out pauses like no one's business, and it's really working. Salespersons are talking more. They fill in the gap for me; they give me more information; they tell me more of their needs; and they go into just a little more depth without me having to ask another question.

I just hope that once Mike fits my new teeth on Friday, I continue with this new habit of mine.

What about you? Do you pause enough? If you had to pause more often, what benefits would it bring to your selling and coaching? I bet it would make a difference, but please don't go having dental implants to ensure you pause more. The pain's just far too much.

Coach's Toolbox – Building a Rapport

What is empathy?

I have two sons separated by two years, very similar in looks but you couldn't get two more different characters. One is reserved, effortlessly sensitive, worries about people all the time, and can spot a personal feeling a mile away even in camouflage.

My other son is completely oblivious to people's feelings, beliefs, and opinions, and is always the centre of attention and very talkative. Not that he's a bad boy, just different.

I know which one is going to be the natural salesperson.

You see, salespeople, coaches, team leaders, sales support teams all need to be sensitive to other people's situations. They need to show empathy to salespersons' positions in order to gain rapport and sell successfully. Empathy can be defined as knowing how people think, what's going on in their world without necessarily agreeing with them. And I firmly believe that this skill can be learnt, so there is hope for my son.

There are two steps to having empathy with salespersons.

1. Step one is being aware of their situation.

2. Step two is acknowledging that you are aware.

Remember to go to step two as people can't guess that you understand them; you have to make it known.

Here are nine practical tips to turn up your empathy volume by being aware of their situation and then showing that you're responsive.

1st, 2nd, 3rd Positioning

This little technique comes from NLP. First position is when you're in your own world appreciating and seeing things from your own point of view. This is not empathy with someone else.

Second position is putting yourself in your salesperson's shoes. Literally leaving your body and floating into theirs, metaphorically speaking, of course, unless you've been watching too many late-night horror movies. Seriously though, imagining that you are in their body, feeling their world and experiencing their emotions, is a brilliant first step to take and really does work.

Third position is a little more difficult to get to. Here you come out of both bodies and observe from a neutral position, being able to see the points of view of both you and the salesperson. Real empathy comes from this position. Try it next time. Feel yourself leaving your body. Pop into theirs next to appreciate their point of view, then wander over to a neutral spot and observe both positions.

Read between the lines

I call this level 3 or global listening – it's the ability to read what's not been said, to rely on gut reactions, to use your sixth sense, to use your intuition. That way you can understand where the salesperson is coming from. Level 1 and 2 listening is as far as most of us go – level 1 is selfish listening in that everything you hear gets related to your personal experiences and for your own purposes. Level 2 is listening or active listening and appreciating your salesperson's point of view.

Trust your level 3. Trust your intuition to read between the lines.

Non-verbal clues

Or body language. To be really empathetic you need to be able to read body language so you can read beyond what is being said. People can change the words they use, but they can't hide their body language. Look for clusters of gestures, not isolated ones.

For example, a crossed arm might be because they're cold or are hiding their paunch. It may not mean being negative or hostile. But crossed arms, alongside crossed body and legs, sitting behind a barrier, jerky eye contact, and pacier language would normally mean there's something up in their mind, and it's not good.

Lower your voice tone

A lower voice pitch is more empathetic. Learn to deepen your tone and people will warm to you sooner. Do ensure your vocals have a good range though; no one wants to listen to someone who is monotone in their delivery.

Listen more

Most salespeople appreciate this but three things you can do to listen with empathy is to paraphrase, mirror language, and use silence more. Paraphrasing asks that you use the salesperson's language and words when summarising. Occasionally repeat back one or two words and raise your voice as you say them to indicate a subtle question. This will get the salesperson to say more. And silence is the best way to let your salesperson say how it is, especially on the phone. I always believe that phone operators would become comfortable with a few seconds of silence so long as there is a purpose to this.

Tell stories

Tell stories during your coaching. Use stories to prove your expertise, to demonstrate your product's uniqueness, in fact any part of the sales process can be enlivened with a story. Now when you tell a story a strange thing happens in the salesperson's mind. They translate the story into their world as if they were in the story. This helps to show them that you are like them, you share similar ideals. People love a story. It's something granted to us as children and we never lose the irresistibility of a tale.

Rapport

Is having something in common with someone, where you are both in tune with each other and can see each other's point of view. You just seem to get on. This normally happens over time. You know when you're with a friend because silence doesn't feel uncomfortable; you just feel relaxed. Friends have deep rapport – they share many aspects of their lives. They think the same much of the time, have things in common, laugh together, and often move in line in more ways than they think.

Rapport is something you can accelerate with salespersons to help build empathy. The quickest and easiest way to do this is to deliberately become like them in some subtle ways. Learn to match them in physical ways. Mirror their body language, positioning; match their voice pace and tone; do this subtly and don't mimic. It's definitely worth practising as it does work.

Empathy gestures

Showing empathy with your body language is something that women are far better at than men. My daughter, who is eight next month, has this completely tied up. She knows when to turn on the empathy charm with Daddy to get what she wants. One of her weapons is head tilt. Bethan uses this when she wants to show lots of empathy with my situation and simply tilts her head sideways. This has a magical effect on the person talking and shows deep empathy.

Try this yourself.

Other empathy-creating gestures are smiles, eye contact, open body language, hands to face to indicate deep listening and thinking about your situation.

Reflective statements

Are really useful little phrases that tell your salesperson that you see where they're coming from. You may not necessarily agree with them, but you appreciate their point of view. That's empathy and not being a "yes" man or woman. Some examples:

"I understand what you're saying."

"I can appreciate how you feel about that."

"I've been through that as well, and it was terrible."

"I see where you're coming from."

"Gosh that must be awful."

So there we have my nine tips to show more empathy with your salesperson – a particularly important skill for salespeople or anyone who deals with people as part of their profession. Some people are natural at it – most of us have to learn it though – these nine tips can help you do just that.

Rapport is Common Ground

A couple of years ago I lived on a typical family estate with three- and four-bedroom homes, each with three children, two dogs, and one barbeque. Every November I received a box of poppies from the Royal British Legion, and I would knock on doors to see how many poppies I could sell.

Each year I raised a consistent £21.79.

POPPY APPEAL

Thank you very much for helping our Appeal.
In this district we collected

£ 5087·91

of which

£ 21·79

was collected by you.
Without your help, we would be unable to
continue our welfare and benevolent work.
Thank you again.
I hope you – and perhaps your friends
– will be able to help us next year.

Yours sincerely

Janet hins

Local Honorary Organiser

Remembrance painting by Maureen Lipman in aid of the Poppy Appeal

Mr. & Mrs. Archer
54 Courtney Close
Stone hills
Tewkesbury
Glos.

People weren't reticent about buying poppies. After all, it's an amazing cause. The problem was that many people had already bought their poppy or had signed up to a standing order or always bought one from a favourite seller. So I had to be happy with my £35.

But one year I decided to try a different tactic and thought about building a rapport with my salespersons. At the time my son Lewis was aged five and actually rather cute. He's now turned into a teenager so it's now rather frightening.

I decided to take him with me, so I decked him out with the posters of rank, a box of poppies around his waist, and a cute bobble hat.

And what happened next was amazing.

The first door I knocked on, the man of the house came to the door, looked at me, and quickly realized that I was selling poppies, then he glanced at Lewis and I could read the man's mind. "Ah", he thought, "this man is selling poppies…I already have my poppy…how can I turn him down? But hold on…he has a son about the age of my son…he's a dad like me…we have something in common…I like this man…he's just like me…where's my wallet?"

That night I made £87.19. Same road, same houses, same people. But I quadrupled my takings.

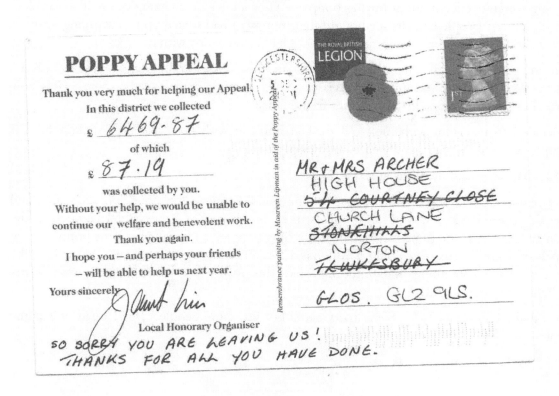

The simple fact was that I was showing my salespersons that I was the same as them; I was building a common ground. You see, people like to deal with people who are the same as them and have done so for thousands of years.

It may not be fair but it's true. People like to deal with people who are the same as them.

The first thing they teach you in sales training school is to find something in common with your salesperson and talk about this. In fact, Dale Carnegie made this famous in his book *How to Win Friends and Influence People,* which was one of the first non-fiction books (outside of college) I ever read.

Something else you can easily do is to become more like your salesperson and the way they are. Pick up on one or two aspects of them and match these. This will build a strong initial rapport.

When face-to-face with salespersons, we can pick up on their body language, seating position, gestures, eye contact, energy levels, conversation…and copy one or two of these. Don't make it too obvious maybe have a time lapse of a few seconds. Possibly sit like they are sitting and copy the amount of eye contact they give you and slow down or speed up to match their energy levels.

When not face-to-face, when on the telephone, you can pick up on aspects of their voice such as speed, volume, tone, rhythm.

Try to follow a couple of aspects of their voice, such as their pace and maybe their tone. You'll be amazed as to the effect it'll have. Your salesperson will feel you are a little like them and will warm to you more.

With a rapport built, you can then concentrate on coaching.

Matching and Mirroring

We mentioned earlier that people like people who are like themselves. It may not be fair, but it is certainly true. We choose our friends, partners, and acquaintances from those people who view things in the same way as we do.

One of the surest and often quickest methods to build a rapport with your coachee is to match them physically. This is well-known and documented, and many people get it wrong, make fools of themselves, and stop doing it. It needs to be subtle and natural and then it works. It really does work.

Matching posture

Match general posture and positioning, not each and every arm movement. Observe your client carefully and gradually move your posture to match theirs. Lean back, sideways, or whatever is appropriate to mirror them. Don't worry about arm movements or crossing of limbs – just go for the basic posture.

Matching energy levels

Then match pace. Are they fast and energetic or slow and cumbersome? Match your pace alongside theirs. More or less of the coffee helps here! Seriously though, have you ever dealt with someone who has a naturally slow pace?

Hard work, isn't it? And vice versa too. But when we're dealing with someone with the same pace, it makes the meeting so much more fruitful.

Matching pace

More experienced matchers then go for breathing patterns and match these. This is a great way to ensure you are able to match their pace as well since the two go together.

Have you ever been in a crowd of people singing a chant or a song, maybe at a rock concert singing along to the chorus? Think back now and just know that whilst you sing, your breathing patterns are like everyone else's and a phenomenal rapport exists in the crowd.

Matching voice

Then comes voice. There's so much you can do to match people's voice, and when you're on the telephone, this is pretty much all you can match. Try to match their voice speed and tone. Do they speak high or low? Try it. It does produce a very amicable conversation between two like-minded people.

Old Trafford and Rapport

One of the advantages of your favourite Premiere League Football team playing erratically is that you can buy tickets for home matches. And so this happened for me at Manchester United's Old Trafford ground.

With my two teenage sons, we ventured to Manchester with our tickets for the first time. Unfortunately we were unable to secure three consecutive seats, my two boys sat next to each other but I was a couple of seats behind them on my own.

However, we were amongst fellow fans, and I soon became ensconced in conversation about Manchester United past and present with my two adjoining new friends. We spoke about Eric Cantona's brilliance, Sparky's incisiveness in attack and Steve Bruce's staunch defensiveness. Plus Schmeichel's antics in front of goal.

We were all soon best buddies.

Doesn't it just prove the value of common ground? I know it's a cliché, but do you still seek common ground with your customers and clients. It's one of the rapport building techniques that will live forever.

Didn't Oasis want to "Live Forever"?

Enough of the Manchester connections, my friends in Liverpool will never let me live that down. Oh I forgot, we won the match 1:0, very rare for Manchester United at the moment.

A Unique Rapport Building Technique

I'm going to combine two very clever techniques from NLP into one mesmerising simple tactic to influence someone.

Let me explain how.

One of the quickest ways to gain rapport with someone is to offer a compliment. Something genuine and meaningful. This has been reported well before NLP was even mentioned; Dale Carnegie mentioned it in his book in the early 20th century.

Yesterday I was working in Dubai for a bank and helping their sales advisers become even more effective in selling. One man was presenting in the classroom and I particularly liked his jacket. It was a local design. A shalwar waistcoat. I thought it was elegant, very tasteful and fitted the occasion.

I genuinely thought so and later bought one in the shopping mall.

At the time I complimented him and said how handsome it made him look. He "purred"

And at the same time I went to touch his shoulder as this is an anchor which I wanted to associate with the moment for him.

The whole group warmed to me and we enjoyed the rest of our time together. As we all departed the training my new friend came up to shake my hand. As I did so I touched his shoulder once more, re-igniting the compliment and the warm feeling he had from earlier. He smiled like a Cheshire cat and we are now friends on facebook and Linked in contacts.

So combine a compliment with a subtle touch anchor to cement the moment and bring it back just by firing the anchor later.

Marvellous and so simple.

Yawning and Rapport

We've known for ages that a yawn is contagious. Someone in the group yawns and someone will yawn in return often instantaneously or within 5 minutes. The reason, we also know, is down to the want to be alike, to be the equal, to create similarity.

Researcher's in Italy's Pisa University found that the "yawn transmission" was quicker amongst those that already had rapport – close friends and lovers.

The study, is based on a rigorous, behavioural data collection carried out for over one year on more than 100 adults, corresponding to more than 400 "yawning couples". People have been observed in a wide array of natural contexts: during meals, on the train, at work, etc. Observations, carried out in Italy and Madagascar, have involved people of different nationalities, and with a different degree of familiarity: strangers and acquaintances (colleagues and friends of friends), friends, kin (parent/offspring, grandparent/grandchild, and siblings), and mates.

So it's been scientifically proved that people who like other people want to be the same and that building a rapport can be accelerated by matching and mirroring the person you want to build rapport with.

So next time you're in a situation where rapport will move the relationship further in the right direction follow this 5 minute induction whilst engaging in your first conversation.

- Shake hands with the person to calibrate their energy levels, and match energy

- Matching energy will allow you to match their voice – tone and pace.

- Calibrate their face first – smile, expressions and amount of eye contact – and match this

- Go peripheral in your vision to observe their overall physiology – body language – posture, position and match this.

- If their posture changes, delay the match for about 20 seconds

- Now pick up their gestures they use when speaking, notice them carefully and match these but only when you talk.

- When you have the rapport, you'll know inside, to test you could alter your physiology a little and watch as they match you.

And if they yawn…don't match this instead end the meeting because you're boring them

Coach's Toolbox – Recordkeeping

Why do we need records?

It's often been said that, "If it's not written down it never happened." Now this probably emanates from an extremely risk-averse company, possibly highly regulated. However, it is true. There needs to be an element of records maintained so you can coach your salespeople appropriately, follow up where necessary, and create a plan in the first place.

But we don't want to be paralysed with forms and paperwork so let me show you how I maintain records for my coaching sessions.

What records are needed when sales coaching?

It's useful to split the coaching sessions into three parts to examine the recordkeeping needed.

- Pre-coaching
- Coaching session
- Post-coaching

Pre-coaching records

Development needs

The most important record would be the development plan for the salesperson. Without this we're not going to be able to target our coaching efforts. In corporations, there will be an appraisal document or an annual development log which should be owned by the salesperson, not you. Many companies call these Personal Development Plans (PDPs), and they often come it the form of a manual where records can be added every time training or development has been received, and that includes your coaching sessions.

PDPs are often digital, forming part of the firm's Learning Management System; all paperwork is digitised and held in the cloud. This is my preferred route.

Performance and learning objectives

You need these, otherwise you have no direction for your training or coaching. Normally contained in the PDP.

Corporate client profiling

This might be slightly "over the top" if you're coaching your own salespeople, but if your role as a coach becomes more executive sales coaching, or you're taking on the responsibilities for a major coaching exercise with one salesperson, it's useful to have the profiling done with your salesperson. I'm going to show you what mine looks like later in this chapter.

Contract

Some coaches go overboard with the contract. I believe a contract can be verbal as well as written, and it needs to cover aspects such as:

- How I should coach you

- What you expect from the sessions

- What I would want from you

And such like. In my coaching profiling tool, we look at this facet.

Agenda/timetable

This is definitely required if you're doing field-based coaching and intend to spend a day with one of your salespeople. Professionals just need it.

Coaching session records

Observation evidence

If you're observing a live client meeting, you'll want to capture evidence and notes on what is said and done to help in your feedback later. Many companies provide these as templates, but a piece of blank paper will do. I like to use the "T" system. Draw a large T on your blank paper, mark the left column positives and the right column negatives, and use this to jot down the client sales call and how well the salesperson performed.

Record of the conversation

The actual session will result in records being created. The danger is that the recordkeeping takes over from the coaching itself. I've seen it. The coach is too busy completing his company's preferred template and action planner, that his eye contact leaves the salesperson who becomes distinctly disengaged regarding the whole process as a form-filling exercise with little value.

By all means, write down what's been discussed although I like to audio record afterwards and mindmap what we're discussing. More on these two later in this chapter.

Records post-coaching

Try not to spend too much time writing up the notes; it'll put you off coaching forever. You do need notes on the actions decided and the next steps the salesperson committed to. Make sure these are kept in the cloud or in the PDP

Mindmapping your coaching session

Traditionally, we are taught to make notes, write, and think on paper in a linear fashion. In other words, the lines on the page structure us. Whilst this method may create "good" or "neat" notes, problems do exist using this method:

- It imposes order on thought.

- It imposes a logical sequence.

- It is long-winded and slow.

- It is boring.

- Items are likely to be missed.

If your brain is to relate the information most efficiently, the information must be structured in such a way as to aid thought and recall.

Advantages of Mindmaps

I use mindmaps all the time when I'm coaching salespeople. They allow me to capture thoughts and conversations without my eye contact leaving them. They're quick, often visual, and hold keywords rather than long sentences. They help me achieve my aims of a two-way conversation where I'm able to really listen to them.

A mindmap has a number of advantages over the linear form of note taking.

- The centre with the main idea is more clearly defined.

- The relative importance of each idea is clearly indicated. More important ideas will be nearer the centre, and less important ideas will be nearer the edge.

- The links between the concepts will be immediately recognisable because of their proximity and connection.

- Therefore, recall and review will be both more effective and more rapid.

- The nature of the structure allows for the easy addition of new information without messy scratching out or squeezing in, etc.

Mindmapping laws

- Start with a central image - this conjures up creative thought whilst significantly increasing memory:

- Use images throughout the map - (arrows, pictures, develop your own code)

- Words - printed - for reading back.

- The printed words should be on lines, and each line should be connected to other lines.

- Colour - to enhance memory and stimulate the thought process.

- Write fast and as freely as possible.

The basic idea is to print everything that your mind generates and let the map generate more ideas. This method overcomes all the disadvantages of the linear method. Try reading this mindmap to yourself starting clockwise at one p.m.

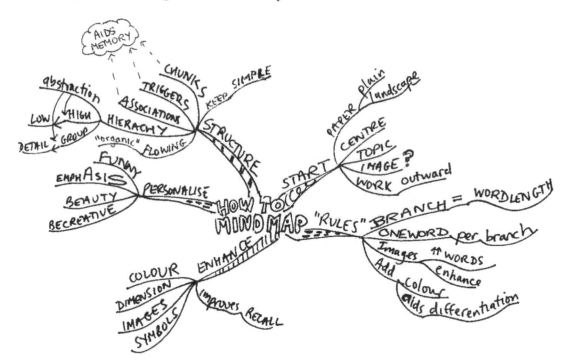

Audio recording the outcomes

Here's a great idea to help you keep records and remember what was done and said at every coaching session you do, and it'll take you just five minutes.

1. Immediately following your coaching session, I mean a minute afterwards, grab your smartphone and click on your favourite audio recording app. My favourite is Nimbus Notes, 'cause it's free.

2. Record everything you recall from the coaching session, what was said and done, in no particular order, just spill your mind.

3. Give it the name of the person you coached and when. Click "send to the cloud".

4. Upload the MP3 to your Dropbox folder specially created to receive the files; you will need to do this before under settings.

5. When back in your office or on your laptop, move it from your Dropbox storage to the client's folder on your hard-drive, which may also be in the cloud.

6. When you are about to do your next coaching meeting with the same client, just play the MP3, and this will flood everything back into your frontal memory, and it's as though you coached them only this morning.

Useful for regular sales coaching, after observations and assessments, field-based coaching sessions, meetings with people, and actions decided.

And it's come to my rescue countless times.

Frontline Sales Coaching

Call Centre Coaching Mastery

Learning styles and coaching

We're all very familiar with Honey and Mumford's Learning Styles piece of work from the 1980s, which describes the four varying styles of learning that we all have. My preferred style is a reflector since I like to look back on my learning events, take my time when learning, think things through, listen to others, and I hate being dropped in at the deep end.

Others might prefer an activist style where being dropped in from a thousand feet would suit them, happy to learn from mistakes, can easily see what their mistakes have been, and can figure out an alternative way in mini seconds. They just seem to want workshops to soar at a hundred miles per hour.

You might prefer a theorist style with a desire to look at all the detail and background to the training topic and to see where theories and models can benefit your learnings.

Or finally, the pragmatist who, by now, has got bored with this piece because they don't see the benefits and how it can help them.

Have you ever used these learning styles to help you maximise your phone-based sales coaching? You may not have thought about it, but it makes perfect sense.

Most phone sales centres or call centres or inside sales operations as our friends across the pond call them, use a variety of coaching interventions. These are:

1. Live side-by-side coaching in the call centre
2. Recorded call coaching in privacy
3. One-to-one coaching with metrics and KPIs
4. Group listening sessions followed by facilitated group discussion on best practice

If you have a choice which one you use with your phone salespeople, then choose the one that fits their learning style.

Side-by-side coaching

For activists – definitely go for live, side-by-side coaching. Here are some tips to make this coaching better for them:

- Decide on a theme to work on during the side-by-sides and listen for this area during your observations.

- Ask your agent for their preferred theme to focus on.

- Focus mostly on feedback and keep it snappy, then ask them what they can do differently.

- Use GROW, but start on reality by giving them feedback on the reality that you just observed, then launch straight into options, giving them a chance to comment.

- Keep the feedback to around two minutes, then get on the next call.

The beauty of live side-by-side is that you get to see the actual challenges they're facing which are non-skill-based, normally system or process, so empathise with them and take some action to improve these.

Recorded feedback sessions

For reflectors – give them more private recorded call coaching sessions. Here are some tips to help you here:

- Give them slightly longer with the "how well did you do" question, look away a little more, give them space to think.

- Let your agent choose the calls to listen to so long as you stipulate a good one and a not-so-good one.

- Don't choose calls randomly; use intelligent speech analytics software to choose keywords, phrases used, attitudes, sentiments, and acoustics.

- Allow your agent to gauge themselves against your best-practice checklist, and then comment afterwards.

- Use silence, non-verbal nods, and lots of matching body language to encourage the reflector to talk… and we do.

- Once some actions start appearing, GROW them naturally and then wrap up with the WHY – where do they need to be? How will I get there and how will you help me?

One-to-one performance coaching

Theorists might prefer the one-to-one coaching with metrics and KPIs to ponder over. Some tips here:

- Let them have the metrics in advance.

- With the exception reports, focus equal time on the above-average performance as opposed to the below-average performance. This is a balanced performance review after all.

- Try and use a balanced scorecard approach to the metrics you measure. You could split these four ways:

1. "How well is your agent serving the salesperson?" – Salesperson satisfaction
2. "How well is your agent performing?" – Operational efficiency
3. "How well is your agent supporting sales?" – Business value
4. "How am I getting the best out of my agents?" – People management

Always have some coaching in the metrics meetings. These are not just assessment and feedback but a chance to spot trends and determine action plans.

Group call listening sessions

Pragmatists might prefer the group interaction, commenting on played-back calls, especially if you have some top performers in the group and keep it punchy. Here are some ideas:

Choose calls carefully, some exemplars and not-such-good calls. Maybe choose a theme upfront.

- Sell the WIIFMs to the agents before you start. (What in it for me's)

- Keep the session to about forty-five minutes.

- Ask them to complete the best-practice checklists.

- Invite everyone for their opinions, but keep this tight. Request one good point and one development area and ban repeating what previous agents have said.

- You don't need to chip in an opinion just for the sake of it; the art is to encourage the agents to comment on their own calls.

My final tip is to ask the agent as to the preferred coaching, what coaching would they want from you to support their growth, and how should the coaching occur? They won't give you pragmatist, theorist, reflector – that's technical jargon for you and me – but they will give you an impression to work on.

Now haven't we breathed a breath of fresh air into Peter and Alan's learning styles?

Twenty-one Tips to Develop Call Centre Coaching

1. To achieve a culture of regular coaching being the way we work around here, here are twenty tips to help you in your busy call centre environment.

2. Have a policy of shutting down email from ten a.m. for all coaches. That way you can swarm over your people and conduct side-by-side coaching, which is what you should be doing ☺.

3. Be clear on the coaching that will work for individual agents. You can use learning styles. For example, activist agents will respond well to side-by-side coaching as they are more than likely to come out with quick actions and responses. Pragmatists will like this too. Reflector agents will cringe with the rapidity of the side-by-side so will prefer the pre-recorded playback sessions in privacy so they can think through how they can improve. Theorist types will also like this, but will want to have access to the calls beforehand. You could get them to choose their best and perceived worst one to analyse, otherwise ensure you use intelligent software to choose the calls for you. Don't spend time trawling through the whole lot. Use technology to help you here.

4. Rather than just one agent listening to their pre-recorded calls, encourage a small group to listen to them and all to add comments and share best practice. Allow each agent to complete your best-practice checklist as they listen to the calls. Then you facilitate an empowering session.

5. Have a "caught you doing something great" emblem to plant on the desktop. One client of mine bought "Wow" lollypops – the large versions – and gave one to an agent when they did something wow.

6. Have a lucky dip bin for great performances. Inside the bin will be booby prizes as well or ones requiring a forfeit.

7. When doing side-by-side coaching, keep the feedback sharpish and precise. Use the session to work on a theme or encourage your agent to suggest a theme before the session starts.

8. Feedback is mostly needed with side-by-side coaching. Don't do too much of the "how would you do that differently". You can leave that for your recorded call coachings.

9. Get a routine going with your agents. Allow them to expect lots of coaching from you. Alternate it with side-by-side coaching followed a few days later with some recorded coaching, some engagement Q&A-type coaching, and then ba side-by-side. Get a routine going.

10. Skills development is a fine outcome of coaching, but use your side-by-side coaching to get an appreciation of the non-skill-based performance inhibitors. Try to understand the real challenges they're under. That'll build empathy.

11. In your recorded call coaching sessions, allow your agent to run the call best-practice checklist themselves on their actual call before giving you feedback.

12. If you're dealing with a low performer, attempt to pick on more than a couple of calls to analyse and coach on. The more the better.

13. After every coaching session, you must have the magical three outcomes. WHY – what, how, you. Your agent should know where they need to be, how they can get there, and what you and the business can do to support them. If they don't know these, then you'll have to spend time GROW'ing them.

14. Use the GROW model by all means, but be aware that it was never designed for a call centre environment. It was originally designed for tennis players and athletes to help them achieve their goals. A tip is to start the GROW model at R = reality, by providing feedback or self-discovered feedback on performance. That way your agent is aware of their current performance where a goal can evolve to improve it.

15. Always, always, always do coaching after any form of assessment. Even if it's billed as a Q&A-type observation, empower these people to do a little bit of coaching afterwards. Never leave observation and assessment in isolation, otherwise it'll get a "police"-type reputation.

16. Ask agents what kind of coaching and development they would like. The type, the duration, how else can you support their skills and development? Naturally your coaching outcomes must be beneficial for the agents, otherwise they just might say, "None please."

17. Have best-practice meetings for five minutes each morning and evening to share best practices and great performances. Stand up and let different agents run them for you.

18. Get your call recording software to burn calls on to a CD or SD card, as many as will fit on, and get in the habit of listening to these on your way home or whilst in the gym. The habit of listening to lots of calls will help you to determine how your agents are doing and what ways they can improve.

19. Have your call best-practice checklist, which contains the process plus all the soft areas needed to perform a great call. Also have your playbook which holds every technique, strategy, and method which brings the call to life, like a best-practice bible. This would need to be added to continually from observations and agents' new ideas.

20. Have a No PC day once a week so you get to surge over your agents all day.

21. Have a balanced scorecard approach for your metrics and measures. Learn to distinguish between lead and lag. Lead measures are those that'll help you judge how the agent is doing and get in some coaching to improve things. Lag measures are after the event, and although coaching may help, the event has happened. A Balanced Scorecard approach could use four measures:

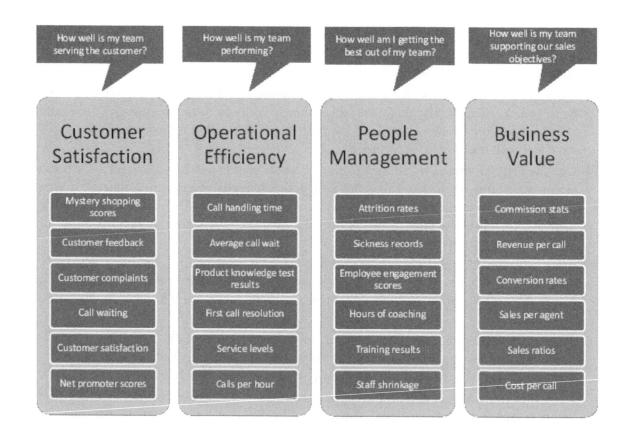